Julie Stafford's
MUFFIN BOOK

Julie Stafford is the highly acclaimed author of the bestselling *Taste of Life* cookbooks, which have sold more than 1.5 million copies worldwide. When her husband, Bruce, was diagnosed as having cancer, Julie became vitally interested in the relationship between diet and disease. She modified her favourite recipes and invented new ones that were low in fat and cholesterol, had no added sugar or salt, were high in fibre, and tasted delicious. Publication of her first *Taste of Life* cookbook followed Bruce's remarkable remission. Julie Stafford's most recent publication, *Juicing for Health*, was released to great acclaim in Australia in 1994 and has subsequently been published in the United Kingdom and the United States.

VIKING

Viking
Penguin Books Australia Ltd
487 Maroondah Highway, PO Box 257
Ringwood, Victoria 3134, Australia
Penguin Books Ltd
Harmondsworth, Middlesex, England
Viking Penguin, A Division of Penguin Books USA Inc.
375 Hudson Street, New York, New York 10014, USA
Penguin Books Canada Limited
10 Alcorn Avenue, Toronto, Ontario, Canada M4V 3B2
Penguin Books (N.Z.) Ltd
182–190 Wairau Road, Auckland 10, New Zealand

10 9 8 7

Photography by Mark Chew
Food styling by Janet Lodge
Typeset in 12/14pt Bembo
Printed in Australia by Australian Print Group, Maryborough,
Victoria

National Library of Australia
Cataloguing-in-Publication

Stafford, Julie.
  Julie Stafford's muffin book: 100 healthy recipes for delicious
  sweet and savoury muffins.

  Includes index.
  ISBN 0 670 85700 9.

  1. Muffins. 2. Low-fat diet – Recipes. 3. Sugar-free diet –
  Recipes. I.   Title. II. title: Muffin book.

641.815

FRONT COVER PHOTOGRAPH

Light, Fluffy Lemon (page 46) and Cherry & Coconut (page 34) muffins.

CONTENTS

Muffins are one of the most versatile foods and suit any occasion: pack them in a school lunchbox, serve them for morning or afternoon tea, take them on a picnic, store them in the freezer and reheat as required, or simply take them from the oven and devour them while they are still warm and full of wonderful flavours.

Savoury muffins – Potato & Herb, Crab & Sun-dried Tomato or Wheat-free Savoury Salmon – are ideal with a soup, to accompany a salad or as a delicious, wholesome meal. Some of my favourite muffins, including Apple & Rhubarb, Marmalade & Banana and Wholemeal Berry Combo, are scrumptious served hot from the oven for breakfast. Muffins, fresh juices and a large platter of fruit provide a high-energy start to your day.

Muffins are a healthy food and can be made even healthier with the addition or exchange of an ingredient. You will note that I use apple juice concentrate as one of the main liquid ingredients throughout this book. I prefer it, for example, to honey, which is approximately 80 per cent sugar; apple juice concentrate is approximately 66 per cent sugar and contains vitamins, minerals and fibre not found in honey. Available commercially, apple juice concentrate can also be made at home by boiling down apple juice to form a syrup; it can be reconstituted, if desired, by adding water.

If you have high blood-cholesterol levels and/or eat a lot of meat and dairy foods, you can cut back on fat and dietary cholesterol by substituting egg whites for whole eggs in all the muffin recipes. The end result will taste just as delicious. Similarly, if you need or wish to avoid dairy foods, low-fat soy milk can replace cow's milk in each of the recipes. Please note, too, that the wheat-free recipes are not just for people with a wheat allergy. Rice flour, soy flour, corn meal and even ground almonds all increase the protein and overall nutritional value of the muffin, but best of all they create sensational flavours.

For those who love the health benefits of a high-fibre, sugar-free diet, but enjoy the occasional taste of a little chocolate, I have even included some chocolate-chip recipes. True health seekers can substitute carob buds for chocolate chips, if they wish. Remember, however, that although carob is caffeine free, it is high in fat.

Although you may think I have exhausted all possible combinations in these 100 muffin recipes, let me share a secret with you: there are endless varieties, depending only on your imagination. You will notice when reading the recipes that a simple method is followed: sift the dry ingredients; add the fresh fruit, dried fruit or vegetables; and combine the liquids (low-fat milk, low-fat soy milk or fresh juices) and eggs before stirring them into the mixture. Once you have followed this method a few times you will see how easy it is to substitute ingredients of your choice to create your own recipes.

I know you will enjoy making and tasting my muffins, especially some of the more unusual ones, for example: Curry, Banana & Sultana; Marsala, Apple & Almond; Apricot, Almond & Corn-meal; Pear, Cheese & Pinenut; Rhubarb & Ginger; and Wheat-free, Orange & Chocolate Chip. Happy muffin making!

SWEET MUFFINS

APPLE & ALMOND MUFFINS

MAKES 12

1½ cups unbleached white self-raising flour
1 cup soy flour
½ teaspoon cinnamon
½ teaspoon mixed spice
½ cup finely chopped almonds
1 x 425 g can unsweetened apple
½ cup grapeseed oil
½ cup apple juice concentrate
¾ cup low-fat milk or low-fat soy milk
4 egg whites or 3 whole eggs

- Preheat the oven to 180°C and lightly grease the muffin tray.

- Sift the flours and spices into a medium-sized bowl and then add the almonds and apple.

- In another bowl, combine the grapeseed oil, apple juice concentrate, milk and egg whites, and beat well.

- Add the egg mixture to the flour and fruit and stir thoroughly.

- Spoon into the muffin tray and bake for 20–25 minutes or until golden brown.

- Remove the muffins immediately from the tray and allow to cool, covered with a tea towel, on a wire rack.

1½ cups unbleached white self-raising flour
½ cup unbleached white plain flour
1 Granny Smith apple, peeled, cored and grated
1 cup sugar-free blackberry jam
½ cup grapeseed oil
1 cup low-fat milk or low-fat soy milk
3 egg whites or 2 whole eggs

APPLE & BLACKBERRY MUFFINS

MAKES 12

- Preheat the oven to 180°C and lightly grease the muffin tray.

- Sift the flours into a medium-sized bowl and add the apple.

- In another bowl, combine the blackberry jam, grapeseed oil, milk and egg whites, and beat well.

- Add the jam mixture to the flour and fruit and stir thoroughly.

- Spoon into the muffin tray and bake for 20–25 minutes or until golden brown.

- Remove the muffins immediately from the tray and allow to cool, covered with a tea towel, on a wire rack.

APPLES

Apples are available all year round and the many varieties provide a host of tastes and textures. They are low in kilojoules, high in vitamin C and an excellent carbohydrate food.

Not only does the pectin in apples add lots of flavour and moisture to a muffin, but it also provides extra natural fibre.

Canned apple (with no added sugar) has the same nutritional value as a fresh apple, so for convenience always keep a couple of cans in your pantry. All other fruits and most spices combine well with apple.

APPLE & DATE MUFFINS

1 cup boiling water
1 cup chopped dates
1 cup chopped Granny Smith apple
1 teaspoon bicarbonate of soda
½ cup grapeseed oil
¼ cup apple juice concentrate
4 egg whites or 3 whole eggs
1 cup unbleached white self-raising flour
1 cup wholemeal self-raising flour

- Pour the boiling water over the dates, apple and bicarbonate of soda in a bowl and leave to stand for 10 minutes.

- Preheat the oven to 180°C and lightly grease the muffin tray.

- In a medium-sized bowl, combine the grapeseed oil, apple juice concentrate and egg whites, and beat well.

- Add the date and apple mixture to the egg mixture.

- Sift the flours into the mixture and stir thoroughly.

- Spoon into the muffin tray and bake for 20–25 minutes or until golden brown.

- Remove the muffins immediately from the tray and allow to cool, covered with a tea towel, on a wire rack.

1 cup boiling water
1 cup chopped dried figs
1½ cups unbleached white self-raising flour
½ cup wholemeal plain flour
2 Granny Smith apples, peeled, cored and diced
1 tablespoon finely grated orange rind
½ cup grapeseed oil
½ cup apple juice concentrate
¾ cup fresh orange juice
3 egg whites or 2 whole eggs

■ Pour the boiling water over the figs in a bowl and leave to stand for 10 minutes.

■ Preheat the oven to 180°C and lightly grease the muffin tray.

■ Sift the flours into a medium-sized bowl and add the fig mixture, apple and orange rind.

■ In another bowl, combine the grapeseed oil, apple juice concentrate, orange juice and egg whites, and beat well.

■ Add the orange juice mixture to the flour and fruit and stir thoroughly.

■ Spoon into the muffin tray and bake for 20–25 minutes.

■ Remove the muffins immediately from the tray and allow to cool, covered with a tea towel, on a wire rack.

APPLE & FIG MUFFINS

MAKES 12

FIGS

The fig tree originated in western Asia and is one of the oldest known cultivated fruit trees. The fruit is high in carbohydrate, rich in fibre and contains magnesium, calcium and iron. Like dates, figs bring sweetness, richness and extra moisture to your muffins and combine especially well with apples, bananas and peaches.

The drying process concentrates the kilojoule value as well as the nutritional value of fruit, so don't over indulge on recipes calling for dried fruits if you want to keep your weight down.

APPLE & PRUNE MUFFINS

MAKES 12

PRUNES

The prune is a dried d'Agen sugar plum. The plum is grown and dried in all corners of the world and traditionally is known for its laxative effect and as an addition to breakfast cereals.

Not only is it highly nutritious and high in fibre, vitamin A, iron and phosphorus, but its flavour also enhances fruit like apples, bananas, peaches and vegetables like pumpkin and sweet potato. Remove the stone before cooking, and if the prunes have dried out, soak them in a little water, fruit juice, port or sherry to moisten them.

1½ cups unbleached white self-raising flour
½ cup wholemeal plain flour
1 teaspoon cinnamon
1 Granny Smith apple, peeled, cored and grated
1 cup stoned and chopped prunes
½ cup grapeseed oil
1 cup unsweetened prune juice
¾ cup low-fat milk or low-fat soy milk
3 egg whites or 2 whole eggs

■ Preheat the oven to 180°C and lightly grease the muffin tray.

■ Sift the flours and spice into a medium-sized bowl and add the apple and prunes.

■ In another bowl, combine the grapeseed oil, prune juice, milk and egg whites, and beat well.

■ Add the prune juice mixture to the flour and fruit and stir thoroughly.

■ Spoon into the muffin tray and bake for 20–25 minutes or until golden brown.

■ Remove the muffins immediately from the tray and allow to cool, covered with a tea towel, on a wire rack.

1½ cups unbleached white self-raising flour
½ cup wholemeal plain flour
1 teaspoon cinnamon
½ teaspoon mixed spice
200 g apples, finely chopped
200 g rhubarb, finely chopped
½ cup grapeseed oil
½ cup apple juice concentrate
¾ cup unsweetened apple juice
3 egg whites or 2 whole eggs

APPLE & RHUBARB MUFFINS

MAKES 12

- Preheat the oven to 180°C and lightly grease the muffin tray.

- Sift the flours and spices into a medium-sized bowl and then add the apple and rhubarb.

- In another bowl, combine the grapeseed oil, apple juice concentrate, apple juice and egg whites, and beat well.

- Add the egg mixture to the flour and fruit and stir thoroughly.

- Spoon into the muffin tray and bake for 20–25 minutes or until golden brown.

- Remove the muffins immediately from the tray and allow to cool, covered with a tea towel, on a wire rack.

APPLE, CURRANT & SPICE MUFFINS

MAKES 12

1½ cups unbleached white self-raising flour
½ cup wholemeal plain flour
2 teaspoons mixed spice
2 Granny Smith apples, cored and chopped
¾ cup currants
½ cup grapeseed oil
½ cup apple juice concentrate
2 teaspoons vanilla essence
¾ cup low-fat milk or low-fat soy milk
3 egg whites or 2 whole eggs

- Preheat the oven to 180°C and lightly grease the muffin tray.

- Sift the flours and spices into a medium-sized bowl and then add the apple and currants.

- In another bowl, combine the grapeseed oil, apple juice concentrate, vanilla, milk and egg whites, and beat well.

- Add the egg mixture to the flour and fruit and stir thoroughly.

- Spoon into the muffin tray and bake for 20–25 minutes or until golden brown.

- Remove the muffins immediately from the tray and allow to cool, covered with a tea towel, on a wire rack.

1½ cups unbleached white self-raising flour
1 cup soy flour
1 teaspoon cinnamon
2 Granny Smith apples, peeled, cored and grated
¼ cup finely chopped walnuts
¼ cup honey
½ cup grapeseed oil
¾ cup apple juice
4 egg whites or 3 whole eggs
12 walnuts, shelled

- Preheat the oven to 180°C and lightly grease the muffin tray.

- Sift the flours and spice into a medium-sized bowl and then add the apple and walnuts.

- In another bowl, combine the honey, grapeseed oil, apple juice and egg whites, and beat well.

- Add the honey mixture to the flour and fruit and stir thoroughly.

- Spoon into the muffin tray and top each muffin with a walnut.

- Bake for 20–25 minutes or until golden brown.

- Remove the muffins immediately from the tray and allow to cool, covered with a tea towel, on a wire rack.

APPLE, HONEY & WALNUT MUFFINS

MAKES 12

WALNUTS

There are fifteen varieties of walnut, the most popular being the yellow–brown.

Walnuts are high in oil and linoleic acid (a polyunsaturated acid). They are also a good source of protein.

Purchase walnuts only as you need them, because once shelled they lose their freshness if not stored in an airtight container in the refrigerator.

Only a small amount of walnut is needed to add a wonderful richness to your muffins or a whole walnut can be added to the top of each muffin before cooking for a dry roasted flavour.

APPLE, OAT & SULTANA MUFFINS

MAKES 12

6 Granny Smith apples, peeled, cored and diced
boiling water
2 cups oat bran
2 cups wholemeal plain flour
1½ tablespoons baking powder
2 teaspoons cinnamon
2 teaspoons mixed spice
1 cup sultanas
grated rind of 1 lemon
½ cup grapeseed oil
½ cup apple juice concentrate
¾ cup fresh orange juice
¼ cup lemon juice
3 egg whites

■ Preheat the oven to 180°C and lightly grease the muffin tray.

■ Cover the apple with boiling water in a bowl for 5 minutes and then drain.

■ Place the oat bran in a medium-sized bowl and sift the flour, baking powder and spices into it. Mix together.

■ Add the apple, sultanas and lemon rind to the dry ingredients.

■ In another bowl, combine the grapeseed oil, apple juice concentrate, orange and lemon juices and add to the flour and apple mixture.

■ Lightly beat the egg whites and gently fold through the mixture.

■ Spoon into the muffin tray and bake for 25–30 minutes or until golden brown.

■ Remove the muffins immediately from the tray and allow to cool, covered with a tea towel, on a wire rack.

1½ cups unbleached white self-raising flour
½ cup unbleached white plain flour
1 teaspoon cinnamon
1 teaspoon ground cardamom
½ teaspoon nutmeg
½ teaspoon ground cloves
1 x 425 g can unsweetened apple
½ cup grapeseed oil
⅓ cup apple juice concentrate
2 teaspoons vanilla essence
¾ cup low-fat milk or low-fat soy milk
3 egg whites or 2 whole eggs

APPLE SPICE MUFFINS

MAKES 12

- Preheat the oven to 180°C and lightly grease the muffin tray.

- Sift the flours and spices into a medium-sized bowl and add the apple.

- In another bowl, combine the grapeseed oil, apple juice concentrate, vanilla, milk and egg whites, and beat well.

- Add the egg mixture to the flour and apple and stir thoroughly.

- Spoon into the muffin tray and bake for 20–25 minutes or until golden brown.

- Remove the muffins immediately from the tray and allow to cool, covered with a tea towel, on a wire rack. (See colour plate opposite page 43.)

EXTRA MOIST APPLE SPICE MUFFINS

MAKES 12

UNBLEACHED WHITE FLOUR

This flour is similar to white flour but it has not been through the bleaching process. Bleaching — the addition of a chemical called benzoyl peroxide — has no purpose other than to make the flour appear whiter in colour and is another example of how foods are being chemically interfered with simply to be visually pleasing. Ironically, flour naturally bleaches when stored.

1 cup unbleached white self-raising flour
1 cup wholemeal plain flour
1 teaspoon cinnamon
½ teaspoon mixed spice
¼ teaspoon nutmeg
2 x 425 g cans unsweetened apple
½ cup grapeseed oil
½ cup apple juice concentrate
¾ cup low-fat milk or low-fat soy milk
3 egg whites or 2 whole eggs

■ Preheat the oven to 180°C and lightly grease the muffin tray.

■ Sift the flours and spices into a medium-sized bowl and add the apple.

■ In another bowl, combine the grapeseed oil, apple juice concentrate, milk and egg whites, and beat well.

■ Add the egg mixture to the flour and apple and stir thoroughly.

■ Spoon into the muffin tray and bake for 20–25 minutes or until golden brown.

■ Remove the muffins immediately from the tray and allow to cool, covered with a tea towel, on a wire rack.

¾ cup corn meal
1¼ cups unbleached white self-raising flour
1 x 425 g can unsweetened apricots in
    natural juice
½ cup flaked almonds
½ cup grapeseed oil
2 tablespoons apple juice concentrate
2 teaspoons vanilla essence
¼ cup fresh lemon or orange juice
3 egg whites or 2 whole eggs

APRICOT, ALMOND & CORN-MEAL MUFFINS

MAKES 12

- Preheat the oven to 180°C and lightly grease the muffin tray.

- Place the corn meal in a medium-sized bowl and sift in the flour. Mix together.

- Drain the apricots, reserving 1 cup juice. Chop the apricots and add to the flour and corn meal with the flaked almonds.

- In another bowl, combine the apricot juice, grapeseed oil, apple juice concentrate, vanilla essence, citrus juice and egg whites, and beat well.

- Add the egg mixture to the flour and apricot mixture and stir thoroughly.

- Spoon into the muffin tray and bake for 20–25 minutes or until golden brown.

- Remove the muffins immediately from the tray and allow to cool, covered with a tea towel, on a wire rack.

APRICOT & COCONUT STREUSEL MUFFINS

MAKES 12

WHOLEMEAL FLOUR
This flour is milled from the whole wheat grain with a large proportion of the outer husk remaining in the finished product. It adds texture, a nutty flavour, and essential fibre to your muffins. Wholemeal flour contains more minerals and vitamins than white flour. It is an excellent source of niacin, iron and magnesium, with smaller amounts of protein and zinc.

1½ cups unbleached white self-raising flour
½ cup wholemeal plain flour
½ cup shredded coconut
400 g fresh apricots, stoned and finely chopped
½ cup grapeseed oil
½ cup apple juice concentrate
¾ cup fresh orange juice
3 egg whites or 2 whole eggs
1 teaspoon cinnamon
2 tablespoons finely chopped shredded coconut

- Preheat the oven to 180°C and lightly grease the muffin tray.

- Sift the flours into a medium-sized bowl and add the coconut and apricots.

- In another bowl, combine the grapeseed oil, apple juice concentrate, orange juice and egg whites, and beat well.

- Add the orange juice mixture to the flour and fruit and stir thoroughly.

- Spoon into the muffin tray.

- Combine the cinnamon and chopped coconut and sprinkle a little on top of each muffin.

- Bake for 20–25 minutes or until golden brown.

- Remove the muffins immediately from the tray and allow to cool, covered with a tea towel, on a wire rack.

EXTRA MOIST BANANA & RAISIN MUFFINS

MAKES 12

¾ cup boiling water
1 teaspoon bicarbonate of soda
1 cup raisins
1 cup mashed banana
½ cup grapeseed oil
½ cup apple juice concentrate
3 egg whites or 2 whole eggs
1½ cups unbleached white self-raising flour
½ cup unbleached white plain flour
½ cup finely chopped walnuts (optional)

- Combine the boiling water, bicarbonate of soda and raisins in a bowl and leave to stand for 10 minutes.

- Preheat the oven to 180°C and lightly grease the muffin tray.

- In another bowl, combine the banana, grapeseed oil, apple juice concentrate and egg whites, and beat well.

- Stir the raisins and their liquid into the banana mixture.

- Sift the flours into the mixture and stir to combine.

- Spoon into the muffin tray and sprinkle chopped walnuts on top of each muffin, if desired.

- Bake for 20–25 minutes or until golden brown.

- Remove the muffins immediately from the tray and allow to cool, covered with a tea towel, on a wire rack.

BANANA & APRICOT MUFFINS

1 cup unbleached white self-raising flour
1 cup wholemeal plain flour
½ teaspoon mixed spice
½ cup finely chopped dried apricots
1 cup mashed banana
½ cup grapeseed oil
½ cup apple juice concentrate
¾ cup low-fat milk or low-fat soy milk
4 egg whites or 3 whole eggs

- Preheat the oven to 180°C and lightly grease the muffin tray.

- Sift the flours and spice into a medium-sized bowl and add the apricots.

- In another bowl, combine the mashed banana, grapeseed oil, apple juice concentrate, milk and egg whites, and beat well.

- Add the banana mixture to the flour and fruit and stir thoroughly.

- Spoon into the muffin tray and bake for 20–25 minutes or until golden brown.

- Remove the muffins immediately from the tray and allow to cool, covered with a tea towel, on a wire rack.

¾ cup corn meal
1¼ cups unbleached white self-raising flour
2½ teaspoons baking powder
3 bananas, peeled and chopped
½ cup sultanas
1 tablespoon grated orange rind
½ cup grapeseed oil
½ cup apple juice concentrate
¾ cup low-fat milk or low-fat soy milk
3 egg whites or 2 whole eggs

- Preheat the oven to 180°C and lightly grease the muffin tray.

- Place the corn meal in a medium-sized bowl and sift in the flour and baking powder. Mix together.

- Add the banana, sultanas and orange rind to the flour and corn meal.

- In another bowl, combine the grapeseed oil, apple juice concentrate, milk and egg whites, and beat well.

- Add the egg mixture to the flour and fruit mixture and stir thoroughly.

- Spoon into the muffin tray and bake for 20–25 minutes or until golden brown.

- Remove the muffins immediately from the tray and allow to cool, covered with a tea towel, on a wire rack.

BANANA & CORN-MEAL MUFFINS

MAKES 12

BANANAS

Bananas, grown in the world's tropical regions, are a good source of vitamin C, contain moderate amounts of fibre and iron, and are especially high in potassium. Bananas are available all year round and although delicious when raw, their best flavour comes when cooked.

Like apples, bananas go well with most other fruits. Adding different spices or a little orange or lemon rind really enhances their overall flavour. Pecan nuts, walnuts or macadamia nuts also combine well with bananas.

BANANA & GINGER MUFFINS

MAKES 12

1½ cups unbleached white self-raising flour
½ cup wholemeal plain flour
3 bananas, peeled and chopped
2 tablespoons finely chopped glacé ginger
½ cup grapeseed oil
½ cup apple juice concentrate
¾ cup fresh orange juice
4 egg whites or 3 whole eggs

- Preheat the oven to 180°C and lightly grease the muffin tray.

- Sift the flours into a medium-sized bowl and add the banana and glacé ginger.

- In another bowl, combine the grapeseed oil, apple juice concentrate, orange juice and egg whites, and beat well.

- Add the orange juice mixture to the flour and fruit and stir thoroughly.

- Spoon into the muffin tray and bake for 20–25 minutes or until golden brown.

- Remove the muffins immediately from the tray and allow to cool, covered with a tea towel, on a wire rack.

1½ cups unbleached white self-raising flour
½ cup wholemeal plain flour
1 teaspoon cinnamon
2 bananas, peeled and chopped
2 oranges, peeled and chopped
½ cup grapeseed oil
½ cup apple juice concentrate or *honey*
¾ cup fresh orange juice
3 egg whites or *2 whole eggs*

- Preheat the oven to 180°C and lightly grease the muffin tray.

- Sift the flours and spice into a medium-sized bowl and then add the banana and orange.

- In another bowl, combine the grapeseed oil, apple juice concentrate, orange juice and egg whites, and beat well.

- Add the orange juice mixture to the flour and fruit and stir thoroughly.

- Spoon into the muffin tray and bake for 20–25 minutes or until golden brown.

- Remove the muffins immediately from the tray and allow to cool, covered with a tea towel, on a wire rack.

BANANA & ORANGE MUFFINS

MAKES 12

BANANA & PASSIONFRUIT MUFFINS

MAKES 12

1½ cups unbleached white self-raising flour
½ cup wholemeal plain flour
2 large bananas, peeled and chopped
flesh of 3 passionfruit
½ cup grapeseed oil
½ cup apple juice concentrate
¾ cup fresh orange juice
3 egg whites or 2 whole eggs

- Preheat the oven to 180°C and lightly grease the muffin tray.

- Sift the flours into a medium-sized bowl and add the banana and passionfruit.

- In another bowl, combine the grapeseed oil, apple juice concentrate, orange juice and egg whites, and beat well.

- Add the orange juice mixture to the flour and fruit and stir thoroughly.

- Spoon into the muffin tray and bake for 20–25 minutes or until golden brown.

- Remove the muffins immediately from the tray and allow to cool, covered with a tea towel, on a wire rack.

PASSIONFRUIT

There are four varieties of passionfruit but the most popular is the purple, which grows best in a subtropical climate.

The purple passionfruit is an excellent carbohydrate food with high levels of vitamin C and fibre. There is really nothing that compares with its sharp, sweet flavour. Just a little added to banana, mango, apricot, peach or apple muffin recipes creates a tropical paradise whenever you desire!

1½ cups unbleached white self-raising flour
½ cup unbleached white plain flour
½ teaspoon cinnamon
½ teaspoon nutmeg
½ cup finely chopped walnuts
4 bananas, peeled and chopped
½ cup grapeseed oil
½ cup apple juice concentrate
¾ cup low-fat milk or low-fat soy milk
3 egg whites or 2 whole eggs

BANANA & WALNUT MUFFINS

MAKES 12

- Preheat the oven to 180°C and lightly grease the muffin tray.

- Sift the flours, cinnamon and nutmeg into a medium-sized bowl and add the walnuts and banana.

- In another bowl, combine the grapeseed oil, apple juice concentrate, milk and egg whites, and beat well.

- Add the egg mixture to the flour and fruit and stir thoroughly.

- Spoon into the muffin tray and bake for 20–25 minutes or until golden brown.

- Remove the muffins immediately from the tray and allow to cool, covered with a tea towel, on a wire rack.

BANANA, DATE & PECAN MUFFINS

MAKES 12

1½ cups unbleached white self-raising flour
½ cup wholemeal plain flour
3 bananas, peeled and chopped
1 teaspoon finely grated lemon rind
1 cup finely chopped dates
½ cup grapeseed oil
½ cup apple juice concentrate
¾ cup low-fat milk or low-fat soy milk
3 egg whites or 2 whole eggs
12 pecan nuts, shelled

- Preheat the oven to 180°C and lightly grease the muffin tray.

- Sift the flours into a medium-sized bowl and then add the banana, lemon rind and dates.

- In another bowl, combine the grapeseed oil, apple juice concentrate, milk and egg whites, and beat well.

- Add the egg mixture to the flour and fruit and stir thoroughly.

- Spoon into the muffin tray and top each muffin with a pecan nut.

- Bake for 20–25 minutes or until golden brown.

- Remove the muffins immediately from the tray and allow to cool, covered with a tea towel, on a wire rack.

1½ *cups unbleached white self-raising flour*
½ *cup wholemeal plain flour*
½ *teaspoon nutmeg*
3 *bananas, peeled and chopped*
½ *cup currants*
¼ *cup honey*
½ *cup grapeseed oil*
¾ *cup low-fat milk or low-fat soy milk*
3 *egg whites or* 2 *whole eggs*

- Preheat the oven to 180°C and lightly grease the muffin tray.

- Sift the flours and spice into a medium-sized bowl and then add the banana and currants.

- In another bowl, combine the honey, grapeseed oil, milk and egg whites, and beat well.

- Add the honey mixture to the flour and fruit and stir thoroughly.

- Spoon into the muffin tray and bake for 20–25 minutes or until golden brown.

- Remove the muffins immediately from the tray and allow to cool, covered with a tea towel, on a wire rack.

BANANA, HONEY & CURRANT MUFFINS

MAKES 12

HONEY

Honey has long been a part of our diets. As a sweetener it is often regarded as being superior to ordinary refined sugar, because where ordinary refined sugar is devoid of nutrients, honey supplies valuable vitamins and minerals.

As with maple syrup, use honey occasionally, realising that it will increase the total kilojoule value of the muffin.

BANANA, OAT & DATE MUFFINS

MAKES 12

2½ cups oat bran
1½ cups wholemeal plain flour
1½ tablespoons baking powder
2 teaspoons mixed spice
1 teaspoon cinnamon
500 g bananas, peeled and finely chopped
100 g dates, finely chopped
½ cup grapeseed oil
½ cup apple juice concentrate
1 cup low-fat milk or low-fat soy milk
3 egg whites

- Preheat the oven to 180°C and lightly grease the muffin tray.

- Place the oat bran in a medium-sized bowl and sift the flour, baking powder and spices into it. Mix together.

- Add the banana and dates to the oat bran and flour mixture and toss to break up and coat well.

- In another bowl, combine the grapeseed oil, apple juice concentrate and milk, and add to the flour and fruit mixture.

- Beat the egg whites until stiff and gently fold through the mixture.

- Spoon into the muffin tray and bake for 25–30 minutes or until golden brown.

- Remove the muffins immediately from the tray and allow to cool, covered with a tea towel, on a wire rack.

2 cups oat bran
2 cups wholemeal plain flour
¼ cup carob powder
1½ tablespoons baking powder
1 teaspoon mixed spice
½ teaspoon ground cloves
400 g ripe bananas, mashed
½ cup grapeseed oil
½ cup apple juice concentrate
1 cup low-fat milk or low-fat soy milk
2 teaspoons vanilla essence
3 egg whites
12 walnuts (optional)

BANANA, OAT, CAROB & CLOVE MUFFINS

MAKES 12

- Preheat the oven to 180°C and lightly grease the muffin tray.

- Place the oat bran in a medium-sized bowl and sift the flour, carob powder, baking powder and spices into it. Mix together.

- In another bowl, combine the banana, grapeseed oil, apple juice concentrate, milk and vanilla essence, and beat well.

- Add the flour and oat bran to the banana mixture in two lots, stirring each time.

- Lightly beat the egg whites and gently fold through the mixture.

- Spoon into the muffin tray and bake for 25–30 minutes or until golden brown.

- Remove the muffins immediately from the tray and allow to cool, covered with a tea towel, on a wire rack.

BLUEBERRY & BANANA MUFFINS

MAKES 12

1½ cups unbleached white self-raising flour
½ cup unbleached white plain flour
1 teaspoon cinnamon or mixed spice
1 cup fresh or frozen blueberries
2 bananas, peeled and chopped
½ cup grapeseed oil
½ cup apple juice concentrate
¾ cup low-fat milk or low-fat soy milk
3 egg whites or 2 whole eggs

- Preheat the oven to 180°C and lightly grease the muffin tray.

- Sift the flours and spice into a medium-sized bowl and add the blueberries and banana.

- In another bowl, combine the grapeseed oil, apple juice concentrate, milk and egg whites, and beat well.

- Add the egg mixture to the flour and fruit and stir thoroughly.

- Spoon into the muffin tray and bake for 20–25 minutes or until golden brown.

- Remove the muffins immediately from the tray and allow to cool, covered with a tea towel, on a wire rack.

1½ cups unbleached white self-raising flour
½ cup wholemeal plain flour
½ cup very finely chopped macadamia nuts
400 g fresh or frozen blueberries
½ cup grapeseed oil
½ cup apple juice concentrate
¾ cup low-fat milk or low-fat soy milk
3 egg whites or 2 whole eggs
extra 6 macadamia nuts, cut in half

BLUEBERRY & MACADAMIA NUT MUFFINS

- Preheat the oven to 180°C and lightly grease the muffin tray.

- Sift the flours into a medium-sized bowl and add the chopped macadamia nuts and blueberries.

- In another bowl, combine the grapeseed oil, apple juice concentrate, milk and egg whites, and beat well.

- Add the egg mixture to the flour and fruit and stir thoroughly.

- Spoon into the muffin tray and top each muffin with half a macadamia nut.

- Bake for 20–25 minutes or until golden brown.

- Remove the muffins immediately from the tray and allow to cool, covered with a tea towel, on a wire rack.

MAKES 12

MACADAMIA NUTS
The macadamia nut is native to the coastal rainforests of Queensland, Australia. It is high in oil, being mainly unsaturated fat, and is a good source of fibre. The rich, almost buttery flavour of the macadamia nut is enhanced when cooked: finely chopped and added to the mixture to complement other ingredients, or as a whole nut added to the top of a muffin before cooking.

BLUEBERRY, OAT & PINEAPPLE MUFFINS

MAKES 12

2 cups oat bran
2 cups unbleached white plain flour
1½ tablespoons baking powder
1 teaspoon cinnamon
1 teaspoon mixed spice
1 teaspoon ground ginger
1 x 440 g can unsweetened pineapple pieces
200 g fresh or frozen blueberries
¼ cup water
½ cup grapeseed oil
½ cup apple juice concentrate
2 teaspoons vanilla essence
3 egg whites

- Preheat the oven to 180°C and lightly grease the muffin tray.

- Place the oat bran in a medium-sized bowl and sift the flour, baking powder and spices into it. Mix together.

- Drain the pineapple, reserving ¾ cup juice, and chop. Add the pineapple and the blueberries to the flour mixture.

- In another bowl, combine the pineapple juice, water, grapeseed oil, apple juice concentrate and vanilla, and beat well.

- Add the pineapple juice mixture to the flour and fruit and fold through.

- Beat the egg whites until stiff and gently fold through the mixture.

- Spoon into the muffin tray and bake for 25–30 minutes or until golden brown.

- Remove the muffins immediately from the tray and allow to cool, covered with a tea towel, on a wire rack.

2 cups oat bran
2 cups unbleached white plain flour
1½ tablespoons baking powder
1 teaspoon cinnamon
1 teaspoon mixed spice
1 teaspoon ground ginger
400 g fresh or frozen blueberries
½ cup grapeseed oil
½ cup apple juice concentrate
1 cup low-fat milk or low-fat soy milk
2 teaspoons vanilla essence
3 egg whites

BLUEBERRY OAT MUFFINS

MAKES 12

- Preheat the oven to 180°C and lightly grease the muffin tray.

- Place the oat bran in a medium-sized bowl and sift the flour, baking powder and spices into it. Mix together.

- Add the blueberries to the flour mixture.

- In another bowl, combine the grapeseed oil, apple juice concentrate, milk and vanilla essence and add to the flour and blueberry mixture.

- Beat the egg whites until stiff and gently fold through the mixture, trying not to squash the blueberries.

- Spoon into the muffin tray and bake for 25–30 minutes or until golden brown.

- Remove the muffins immediately from the tray and allow to cool, covered with a tea towel, on a wire rack.

BLUEBERRY SOY MUFFINS

MAKES 12

BLUEBERRIES

These plump, small, round, juicy berries, with their sweet–tart taste and purple–blue skin, make the most delicious muffin ingredient. A native of North America, blueberries are an excellent source of vitamin C and have a moderate amount of iron and fibre.

1½ cups unbleached white self-raising flour
1 cup soy flour
400 g fresh or frozen blueberries
½ cup grapeseed oil
½ cup apple juice concentrate
¾ cup low-fat milk or low-fat soy milk
4 egg whites or 3 whole eggs

■ Preheat the oven to 180°C and lightly grease the muffin tray.

■ Sift the flours into a medium-sized bowl and add the blueberries.

■ In another bowl, combine the grapeseed oil, apple juice concentrate, milk and egg whites, and beat well.

■ Add the egg mixture to the flour and fruit and stir thoroughly.

■ Spoon into the muffin tray and bake for 20–25 minutes or until golden brown.

■ Remove the muffins immediately from the tray and allow to cool, covered with a tea towel, on a wire rack.

¾ cup corn meal
1¼ cups unbleached white self-raising flour
2 cups fresh or frozen blueberries
¼ cup finely chopped walnuts
½ cup grapeseed oil
½ cup apple juice concentrate
¾ cup low-fat milk or low-fat soy milk
3 egg whites or 2 whole eggs

- Preheat the oven to 180°C and lightly grease the muffin tray.
- Place the corn meal in a medium-sized bowl and sift the flour into it.
- Add the blueberries and walnuts to the flour and mix together.
- In another bowl, combine the grapeseed oil, apple juice concentrate, milk and egg whites, and beat well.
- Add the egg mixture to the flour and fruit and stir thoroughly.
- Spoon into the muffin tray and bake for 20–25 minutes or until golden brown.
- Remove the muffins immediately from the tray and allow to cool, covered with a tea towel, on a wire rack.

BLUEBERRY, WALNUT & CORN-MEAL MUFFINS

MAKES 12

BRAN & APRICOT MUFFINS

BRAN

Bran is obtained by removing the thin outer layers of the wheat kernel during milling. Its fibre and iron content make it an extremely nutritious addition to any diet.

The fibre is water-insoluble — the opposite to oat bran — and so works differently in the body. Essentially it is the opposite to oat bran — and so associated with the speedy removal of wastes. Because bran can be coarse or fine in texture, depending on the milling process, you may need to add a little extra moisture to your muffin mxture if it is too dry.

1 cup bran
1 cup unbleached white plain flour
3 teaspoons baking powder
½ teaspoon bicarbonate of soda
1 teaspoon cinnamon
1 teaspoon ground ginger
¾ cup finely chopped dried apricots
½ cup grapeseed oil
½ cup maple syrup
¾ cup low-fat milk or low-fat soy milk
3 egg whites or 2 whole eggs

■ Preheat the oven to 180°C and lightly grease the muffin tray.

■ Place the bran in a medium-sized bowl and sift the flour, baking powder, bicarbonate of soda and spices into it.

■ Add the dried apricots to the flour and bran and mix together.

■ In another bowl, combine the grapeseed oil, maple syrup, milk and egg whites, and beat well.

■ Add the maple syrup mixture to the flour and fruit and stir thoroughly.

■ Spoon into the muffin tray and bake for 20–25 minutes or until golden brown.

■ Remove the muffins immediately from the tray and allow to cool, covered with a tea towel, on a wire rack.

1 cup bran
1 cup unbleached white plain flour
3 teaspoons baking powder
½ teaspoon bicarbonate of soda
2 teaspoons cinnamon
1 cup finely chopped raisins
½ cup grapeseed oil
½ cup maple syrup
¾ cup fresh orange juice
3 egg whites or 2 whole eggs

BRAN & MAPLE MUFFINS

● MAKES 12 ●

- Preheat the oven to 180°C and lightly grease the muffin tray.

- Place the bran in a medium-sized bowl and sift the flour, baking powder, bicarbonate of soda and cinnamon into it.

- Add the raisins to the dry ingredients and mix together.

- In another bowl, combine the grapeseed oil, maple syrup, orange juice and egg whites, and beat well.

- Add the maple syrup mixture to the flour and fruit and stir thoroughly.

- Spoon into the muffin tray and bake for 20–25 minutes or until golden brown.

- Remove the muffins immediately from the tray and allow to cool, covered with a tea towel, on a wire rack.

CHERRY & COCONUT MUFFINS

MAKES 12

1½ cups unbleached white self-raising flour
½ cup rolled oats
1 cup shredded coconut
125 g red glacé cherries
½ cup grapeseed oil
½ cup apple juice concentrate
1 cup low-fat milk or low-fat soy milk
2 teaspoons vanilla essence
3 egg whites or 2 whole eggs

- Preheat the oven to 180°C and lightly grease the muffin tray.

- Sift the flour into a medium-sized bowl and add the rolled oats and coconut.

- Rinse the cherries under running water to remove the sugary syrup and then drain. Finely chop the cherries and add to the dry ingredients.

- In another bowl, combine the grapeseed oil, apple juice concentrate, milk, vanilla and egg whites, and beat well.

- Add the egg mixture to flour and fruit and stir thoroughly.

- Spoon into the muffin tray and bake for 20–25 minutes or until golden brown.

- Remove the muffins immediately from the tray and allow to cool, covered with a tea towel rack.

1½ cups unbleached white self-raising flour
½ cup wholemeal plain flour
1 teaspoon cinnamon
½ cup cocoa or carob powder
300 g fresh or frozen blueberries
½ cup grapeseed oil
½ cup apple juice concentrate
¾ cup low-fat milk or low-fat soy milk
3 egg whites or 2 whole eggs

CHOCOLATE BLUEBERRY MUFFINS

MAKES 12

- Preheat the oven to 180°C and lightly grease the muffin tray.

- Sift the flours, cinnamon and cocoa into a medium-sized bowl and add the blueberries.

- In another bowl, combine the grapeseed oil, apple juice concentrate, milk and egg whites, and beat well.

- Add the egg mixture to the flour and fruit and stir thoroughly.

- Spoon into the muffin tray and bake for 20–25 minutes or until golden brown.

- Remove the muffins immediately from the tray and allow to cool, covered with a tea towel, on a wire rack.

CAROB

Carob used in cooking comes from the long pods of the carob tree. It has no significant nutritional value, but its flavour is similar to chocolate; carob is also free of caffeine. Carob buds usually have high levels of added fat and some added sugar so use them sparingly if on a low-fat, sugar-free diet.

CHOCOLATE CHIP MUFFINS

MAKES 12

1½ cups unbleached white self-raising flour
½ cup unbleached white plain flour
¼ cup cocoa or carob powder
¾ cup chocolate chips or carob buds
½ cup grapeseed oil
½ cup apple juice concentrate
1 cup low-fat milk or low-fat soy milk
2 teaspoons vanilla essence
4 egg whites or 3 whole eggs

- Preheat the oven to 180°C and lightly grease the muffin tray.

- Sift the flours and cocoa into a medium-sized bowl and add the chocolate chips.

- In another bowl, combine the grapeseed oil, apple juice concentrate, milk, vanilla essence and egg whites, and beat well.

- Add the egg mixture to the dry ingredients and stir thoroughly.

- Spoon into the muffin tray and bake for 20–25 minutes or until golden brown.

- Remove the muffins immediately from the tray and allow to cool, covered with a tea towel, on a wire rack.

1 cup boiling water
1 cup finely chopped dates
¼ teaspoon bicarbonate of soda
1½ cups unbleached white self-raising flour
½ cup wholemeal plain flour
¼ cup cocoa or carob powder
½ cup grapeseed oil
¼ cup apple juice concentrate
¾ cup low-fat milk or low-fat soy milk
2 teaspoons vanilla essence
3 egg whites or 2 whole eggs

CHOCOLATE DATE MUFFINS

MAKES 12

- Preheat the oven to 180°C and lightly grease the muffin tray.

- Pour the boiling water over the dates in a bowl and add the bicarbonate of soda. Leave to stand for 5 minutes.

- Sift the flours and cocoa into a medium-sized bowl.

- In another bowl, combine the grapeseed oil, apple juice concentrate, milk, vanilla essence and egg whites, and beat well.

- Add the dry ingredients and dates to the egg mixture and stir thoroughly.

- Spoon into the muffin tray and bake for 20–25 minutes or until golden brown.

- Remove the muffins immediately from the tray and allow to cool, covered with a tea towel, on a wire rack.

BAKING POWDER

This fine, white powder, high in sodium but unlike bicarbonate of soda, is an excellent source of calcium and phosphorus. When heated it gives off carbon dioxide that causes the mixture to which it has been added to become aerated or light in texture.

For a sodium-free baking powder combine the following: 2 tablespoons each of cornflour, cream of tartar and potassium bicarbonate (available at chemists). Store this mixture in an airtight container and use about 2 teaspoons for every cup of flour. Many health food stores now sell this product.

CHOCOLATE WHOLEMEAL MUFFINS

MAKES 12

1½ cups unbleached white self-raising flour
1 cup wholemeal plain flour
¼ cup cocoa or carob powder
¼ cup boiling water
1 teaspoon vanilla essence
½ cup grapeseed oil
½ cup apple juice concentrate
¾ cup low-fat milk or low-fat soy milk
4 egg whites or 3 whole eggs
¼ cup flaked almonds (optional)

- Preheat the oven to 180°C and lightly grease the muffin tray.

- Sift the flours into a medium-sized bowl.

- In another bowl, combine the cocoa, boiling water and vanilla essence, and stir well to remove any lumps.

- Add the grapeseed oil, apple juice concentrate, milk and egg whites to the cocoa mixture, and beat well.

- Add the flour to the mixture and stir thoroughly.

- Spoon into the muffin tray and sprinkle flaked almonds on top, if desired.

- Bake for 20–25 minutes or until golden brown.

- Remove the muffins immediately from the tray and allow to cool, covered with a tea towel, on a wire rack.

250 g mixed dried fruit
¼ cup brandy
¾ cup fresh orange juice
½ cup grapeseed oil
½ cup apple juice concentrate
3 egg whites or 2 whole eggs
1½ cups unbleached white self-raising flour
½ cup wholemeal plain flour
1 teaspoon cinnamon
¼ teaspoon ground cloves
¼ teaspoon nutmeg

CHRISTMAS MUFFINS

MAKES 12

- Soak the dried fruit in the brandy in a medium-sized bowl for at least 1 hour or preferably overnight.

- Preheat the oven to 180°C and lightly grease the muffin tray.

- Add the orange juice, grapeseed oil and apple juice concentrate to the dried fruit.

- Beat the egg whites and fold into the fruit mixture.

- Sift the flours and spices into the mixture and stir thoroughly.

- Spoon into the muffin tray and bake for 25–30 minutes or until golden brown.

- Remove the muffins immediately from the tray and allow to cool, covered with a tea towel, on a wire rack.

CORN-MEAL & CURRANT BRAN MUFFINS

MAKES 12

2 cups corn meal
2 cups oat bran
1½ tablespoons baking powder
1 cup currants
1 cup non-fat or low-fat yoghurt
1 cup low-fat milk or low-fat soy milk
½ cup grapeseed oil
½ cup apple juice concentrate
2 teaspoons vanilla essence
3 egg whites

- Preheat the oven to 180°C and lightly grease the muffin tray.

- Combine the corn meal, oat bran, baking powder and currants in a medium-sized bowl and mix well.

- In another bowl, combine the remaining ingredients, except for the egg whites, and add to the corn-meal mixture. Stir thoroughly.

- Lightly beat the egg whites and fold into the mixture.

- Spoon into the muffin tray and bake for 20–25 minutes or until golden brown.

- Remove the muffins immediately from the tray and allow to cool, covered with a tea towel, on a wire rack.

DATE, RUM & PECAN MUFFINS

1½ cups chopped dates
2 tablespoons rum
1 cup unbleached white self-raising flour
½ cup wholemeal plain flour
1 teaspoon cinnamon
½ cup chopped pecan nuts
½ cup grapeseed oil
¼ cup honey or apple juice concentrate
1 cup fresh orange juice
3 egg whites or 2 whole eggs

MAKES 12

- Soak the dates in the rum for at least 1 hour or preferably overnight.

- Preheat the oven to 180°C and lightly grease the muffin tray.

- Sift the flours and spice into a medium-sized bowl and add the dates (and any juice not absorbed) and pecan nuts.

- In another bowl, combine the grapeseed oil, honey, orange juice and egg whites, and beat well.

- Add the orange juice mixture to the flour and fruit and stir thoroughly.

- Spoon into the muffin tray and bake for 20–25 minutes or until golden brown.

- Remove the muffins immediately from the tray and allow to cool, covered with a tea towel, on a wire rack.

DATES

The date is considered, along with the fig, to be the oldest known of all cultivated fruits. It is an excellent energy food because of its carbohydrate value and contains fibre, some iron, magnesium, niacin, folate and vitamin B6.

You can buy dates fresh or dried and either is excellent in muffins. If you find your dates are very hard and dry, soak them overnight in water or, for extra flavour, unsweetened fruit juices, brandy, sherry, port, marsala or rum. Drain off any liquid before using.

Dates combine particularly well with apples, bananas, apricots, pears and oranges.

FIG, ALMOND & PRUNE MUFFINS

MAKES 12

1½ cups unbleached white self-raising flour
½ cup wholemeal plain flour
1 teaspoon mixed spice
1 cup finely chopped dried figs
½ cup flaked almonds
½ cup grapeseed oil
1 cup unsweetened prune juice
¾ cup low-fat milk or low-fat soy milk
3 egg whites or 2 whole eggs

- Preheat the oven to 180°C and lightly grease the muffin tray.

- Sift the flours and spice into a medium-sized bowl and add the figs and almonds.

- In another bowl, combine the grapeseed oil, prune juice, milk and egg whites, and beat well.

- Add the prune juice mixture to the flour and fruit and stir thoroughly.

- Spoon into the muffin tray and bake for 20–25 minutes or until golden brown.

- Remove the muffins immediately from the tray and allow to cool, covered with a tea towel, on a wire rack.

OPPOSITE
Raspberry & Pecan Streusel
Muffin (page 58).

1½ cups unbleached white self-raising flour
½ cup unbleached white plain flour
300 g fresh or frozen blueberries
1 tablespoon finely grated lemon rind
½ cup grapeseed oil
½ cup apple juice concentrate
¾ cup fresh orange juice
4 egg whites or 3 whole eggs

- Preheat the oven to 180°C and lightly grease the muffin tray.

- Sift the flours into a medium-sized bowl and add the blueberries and lemon rind.

- In another bowl, combine the grapeseed oil, apple juice concentrate, orange juice and egg whites, and beat well.

- Add the egg mixture to the flour and fruit and stir thoroughly.

- Spoon into the muffin tray and bake for 20–25 minutes or until golden brown.

- Remove the muffins immediately from the tray and allow to cool, covered with a tea towel, on a wire rack.

LEMON & BLUEBERRY MUFFINS

MAKES 12

OPPOSITE
Apple Spice Muffins (page 11).

LEMON & POPPYSEED MUFFINS

MAKES 12

1½ cups unbleached white self-raising flour
½ cup wholemeal plain flour
¼ cup poppyseeds
1 tablespoon finely grated lemon rind
½ cup grapeseed oil
½ cup apple juice concentrate
½ cup lemon juice
½ cup low-fat milk or low-fat soy milk
4 egg whites or 3 whole eggs

■ Preheat the oven to 180°C and lightly grease the muffin tray.

■ Sift the flours into a medium-sized bowl and add the poppyseeds and lemon rind.

■ In another bowl, combine the grapeseed oil, apple juice concentrate, lemon juice, milk and egg whites, and beat well.

■ Add the lemon juice mixture to the flour and fruit and stir thoroughly.

■ Spoon into the muffin tray and bake for 20–25 minutes or until golden brown.

■ Remove the muffins immediately from the tray and allow to cool, covered with a tea towel, on a wire rack.

½ cup corn meal
1½ cups unbleached white self-raising flour
1 teaspoon ground ginger
1 tablespoon finely grated lemon rind
½ cup finely chopped glacé ginger
1 Granny Smith apple, peeled, cored and grated
½ cup grapeseed oil
½ cup apple juice concentrate
½ cup lemon juice
¼ cup fresh orange juice
3 egg whites or 2 whole eggs

LEMON, GINGER & CORN-MEAL MUFFINS

MAKES 12

- Preheat the oven to 180°C and lightly grease the muffin tray.

- Place the corn meal in a medium-sized bowl and sift the flour and spice into it. Mix together.

- Add the lemon rind, glacé ginger and apple to the dry ingredients.

- In another bowl, combine the grapeseed oil, apple juice concentrate, lemon juice, orange juice and egg whites, and beat well.

- Add the fruit juice mixture to the flour and fruit and stir thoroughly.

- Spoon into the muffin tray and bake for 20–25 minutes or until golden brown.

- Remove the muffins immediately from the tray and allow to cool, covered with a tea towel, on a wire rack.

GLACÉ GINGER
Glacé ginger is cooked ginger that has been dipped in hot water to melt the surface, drained, and then dipped in a very strong sugary syrup to give it a smooth, glossy finish. To remove the syrup and most of the sugar before cooking, run the glacé fruit under warm water and dry on a paper towel.

LIGHT, FLUFFY LEMON MUFFINS

MAKES 12

2 *cups unbleached white self-raising flour*
2 *teaspoons finely grated lemon rind*
½ *cup grapeseed oil*
½ *cup apple juice concentrate*
½ *cup lemon juice*
½ *cup low-fat milk* or *low-fat soy milk*
4 *egg whites* or *3 whole eggs*
12 *macadamia nuts (optional)*

- Preheat the oven to 180°C and lightly grease the muffin tray.

- Sift the flour into a medium-sized bowl and add the lemon rind.

- In another bowl, combine the grapeseed oil, apple juice concentrate, lemon juice, milk and egg whites, and beat well.

- Slowly add the flour and lemon rind a little at a time to the lemon juice mixture and stir thoroughly.

- Spoon into the muffin tray and top each muffin with a macadamia nut, if desired.

- Bake for 20–25 minutes or until golden brown.

- Remove the muffins immediately from the tray and allow to cool, covered with a tea towel, on a wire rack.

1½ cups unbleached white self-raising flour
½ cup wholemeal plain flour
½ cup shredded coconut
1 teaspoon finely grated lemon rind
¼ cup lemon juice
½ cup grapeseed oil
½ cup apple juice concentrate
¾ cup low-fat milk or low-fat soy milk
4 egg whites or 3 whole eggs

- Preheat the oven to 180°C and lightly grease the muffin tray.

- Sift the flours into a medium-sized bowl and add the coconut and lemon rind.

- In another bowl, combine the lemon juice, grapeseed oil, apple juice concentrate, milk and egg whites, and beat well.

- Add the lemon juice mixture to the flour and fruit and stir thoroughly.

- Spoon into the muffin tray and bake for 20–25 minutes or until golden brown.

- Remove the muffins immediately from the tray and allow to cool, covered with a tea towel, on a wire rack.

WHOLEMEAL LEMON & COCONUT MUFFINS

MAKES 12

LEMONS
The lemon is thought to have originated in the south of China, India and Burma. It is now successfully cultivated in many warm coastal areas around the world where it is used to flavour both sweet and savoury cooking.

Like other citrus fruit the lemon is low in kilojoules and high in vitamin C and fibre. Lemon juice can be used as one of the liquids needed in muffin making and lemon rind heightens the flavour of most muffins, especially those including apple, banana, pear, peach, blueberry or zucchini.

MANGO & BANANA MUFFINS

1½ cups unbleached white self-raising flour
½ cup wholemeal plain flour
1 mango, peeled and cubed
1½ bananas, peeled and chopped
½ cup grapeseed oil
½ cup apple juice concentrate
¾ cup low-fat milk or low-fat soy milk
3 egg whites or 2 whole eggs
12 pecan nuts (optional)

MAKES 12

- Preheat the oven to 180°C and lightly grease the muffin tray.

- Sift the flours into a medium-sized bowl and add the mango and banana.

- In another bowl, combine the grapeseed oil, apple juice concentrate, milk and egg whites, and beat well.

- Add the egg mixture to the flour and fruit and stir thoroughly.

- Spoon into the muffin tray and top each muffin with a pecan nut, if desired.

- Bake for 20–25 minutes or until golden brown.

- Remove the muffins immediately from the tray and allow to cool, covered with a tea towel, on a wire rack.

MANGOES

The mango, at its peak in summer, is one of the most delicious tropical fruits. It has a high vitamin A level and lower amounts of iron and vitamin C.

Although my favourite way to eat a mango is simply to peel away the outer skin and devour its fragrant, velvety, smooth flesh, it also cooks well, especially when combined with other fruits, such as bananas and apples. A little sharp cheese in your mango muffin creates a surprisingly flavoursome combination too.

Spices such as cinnamon, ginger and cardamom will complement your mango recipes beautifully.

1½ cups unbleached white self-raising flour
½ cup wholemeal plain flour
3 bananas, peeled and chopped
½ cup unsweetened marmalade
½ cup grapeseed oil
¾ cup fresh orange juice
3 egg whites or 2 whole eggs

MARMALADE & BANANA MUFFINS

MAKES 12

- Preheat the oven to 180°C and lightly grease the muffin tray.

- Sift the flours into a medium-sized bowl and add the banana.

- In another bowl, combine the marmalade, grapeseed oil, orange juice and egg whites, and beat well.

- Add the marmalade mixture to the flour and fruit and stir thoroughly.

- Spoon into the muffin tray and bake for 20–25 minutes or until golden brown.

- Remove the muffins immediately from the tray and allow to cool, covered with a tea towel, on a wire rack.

MARSALA, APPLE & ALMOND MUFFINS

MAKES 12

2 large Granny Smith apples, peeled, cored and
   finely diced
½ cup marsala
1½ cups unbleached white self-raising flour
½ cup wholemeal plain flour
½ cup grapeseed oil
½ cup apple juice concentrate
½ cup low-fat milk or low-fat soy milk
3 egg whites or 2 whole eggs
¼ cup very finely ground almonds
1½ teaspoons cinnamon

- Combine the apple and marsala in a bowl and allow to stand for 1 hour. Drain the apple, reserving the marsala juice.

- Preheat the oven to 180°C and lightly grease the muffin tray.

- Sift the flours into a medium-sized bowl and add the apple.

- In another bowl, combine the marsala juice, grapeseed oil, apple juice concentrate, milk and egg whites, and beat well.

- Add the marsala mixture to the flour and apple and stir thoroughly.

- Spoon into the muffin tray.

- Combine the ground almonds and spice and liberally sprinkle over the top of each muffin.

- Bake for 20–25 minutes or until golden brown.

- Remove the muffins immediately from the tray and allow to cool, covered with a tea towel, on a wire rack.

1½ cups unbleached white self-raising flour
½ cup wholemeal plain flour
1 teaspoon mixed spice
½ teaspoon cinnamon
1 x 425 g can unsweetened peaches in
  natural juice
1 x 425 g can unsweetened apple
½ cup grapeseed oil
¾ cup low-fat milk or low-fat soy milk
3 egg whites or 2 whole eggs

- Preheat the oven to 180°C and lightly grease the muffin tray.

- Sift the flours and spices into a medium-sized bowl.

- Drain the peaches, reserving ½ cup juice, and chop. Add with the apple to the flour.

- In another bowl, combine the peach juice, grapeseed oil, milk and egg whites, and beat well.

- Add the peach juice mixture to the flour and fruit and stir thoroughly.

- Spoon into the muffin tray and bake for 20–25 minutes or until golden brown.

- Remove the muffins immediately from the tray and allow to cool, covered with a tea towel, on a wire rack.

PEACH & APPLE MUFFINS

MAKES 12

UNBLEACHED WHITE FLOUR

This flour is similar to white flour but it has not been through the bleaching process. Bleaching — the addition of a chemical called benzoyl peroxide — has no purpose other than to make the flour appear whiter in colour and is another example of how foods are being chemically interfered with simply to be visually pleasing. Ironically, flour naturally bleaches when stored.

PEAR, OAT & CINNAMON MUFFINS

MAKES 12

OAT BRAN

Oat bran is produced after the whole oat grain has been steamed, flattened and ground. It is an excellent source of soluble fibre and is recognised for its ability to lower blood cholesterol. The water-soluble fibre becomes gel-like in the intestine and binds with the bile acids, which break down cholesterol, causing them to be excreted. The liver responds by draining more cholesterol from the blood to produce more bile, setting up a cycle for ridding the body of excess cholesterol.

Oat bran is an excellent source of iron, thiamin and niacin and contributes a nutty flavour when cooked.

1 cup rolled oats
2 cups oat bran
1 cup unbleached white plain flour
1½ tablespoons baking powder
3 teaspoons cinnamon
¼ cup lemon juice
¾ cup fresh or unsweetened orange juice
½ cup grapeseed oil
½ cup apple juice concentrate
2 teaspoons vanilla essence
400 g pears, cored and diced
3 egg whites

- Preheat the oven to 180°C and lightly grease the muffin tray.

- Place the rolled oats and oat bran in a medium-sized bowl and sift the flour, baking powder and cinnamon into it. Mix together.

- Combine the remaining ingredients, except for the egg whites, in another bowl, and beat well.

- Fold the dry ingredients into the fruit juice mixture and stir thoroughly.

- Beat the egg whites until stiff peaks form and gently fold through the mixture.

- Spoon into the muffin tray and bake for 25–30 minutes or until golden brown.

- Remove the muffins immediately from the tray and allow to cool, covered with a tea towel, on a wire rack.

1½ cups unbleached white self-raising flour
½ cup wholemeal plain flour
1 teaspoon ground ginger
1 x 440 g can crushed, unsweetened pineapple
    in natural juice
½ large mango, peeled and chopped
1 tablespoon finely grated lemon rind
½ cup grapeseed oil
2 tablespoons apple juice concentrate
¼ cup fresh orange juice
3 egg whites or 2 whole eggs

PINEAPPLE & MANGO MUFFINS

MAKES 12

■ Preheat the oven to 180°C and lightly grease the muffin tray.

■ Sift the flours and spice into a medium-sized bowl.

■ Drain the pineapple, reserving 1 cup juice, and add to the flour with the mango and lemon rind.

■ In another bowl, combine the pineapple juice, grapeseed oil, apple juice concentrate, orange juice and egg whites, and beat well.

■ Add the fruit juice mixture to the flour and fruit and stir thoroughly.

■ Spoon into the muffin tray and bake for 20–25 minutes or until golden brown.

■ Remove the muffins immediately from the tray and allow to cool, covered with a tea towel, on a wire rack.

PINEAPPLE, OAT & DATE MUFFINS

MAKES 12

2 cups oat bran
2 cups soy flour or unbleached white plain flour
1½ tablespoons baking powder
2 teaspoons cinnamon
2 x 440 g cans unsweetened pineapple pieces in natural juice
200 g dates, chopped
½ cup grapeseed oil
½ cup apple juice concentrate
2 teaspoons vanilla essence
3 egg whites

- Preheat the oven to 180°C and lightly grease the muffin tray.

- Place the oat bran in a medium-sized bowl and sift the flour, baking powder and cinnamon into it.

- Drain the pineapple, reserving 1 cup juice, and chop.

- In another bowl, combine the pineapple juice, pineapple, dates, grapeseed oil, apple juice concentrate and vanilla.

- Fold the dry ingredients into the fruit mixture in three lots.

- Beat the egg whites until stiff and then fold them through the mixture.

- Spoon into the muffin tray and bake for 25–30 minutes or until golden brown.

- Remove the muffins immediately from the tray and allow to cool, covered with a tea towel, on a wire rack.

1½ cups unbleached white self-raising flour
½ cup unbleached white plain flour
1 teaspoon cinnamon
1 cup fresh or frozen raspberries
2 bananas, peeled and chopped
½ cup grapeseed oil
½ cup apple juice concentrate
¾ cup low-fat milk or low-fat soy milk
3 egg whites or 2 whole eggs

RASPBERRY & BANANA MUFFINS

MAKES 12

- Preheat the oven to 180°C and lightly grease the muffin tray.

- Sift the flours and spice into a medium-sized bowl and add the raspberries and banana.

- In another bowl, combine the grapeseed oil, apple juice concentrate, milk and egg whites, and beat well.

- Add the egg mixture to the flour and fruit and stir thoroughly.

- Spoon into the muffin tray and bake for 20–25 minutes or until golden brown.

- Remove the muffins immediately from the tray and allow to cool, covered with a tea towel, on a wire rack.

RASPBERRY CHOCOLATE MUFFINS

1½ cups unbleached white self-raising flour
½ cup wholemeal plain flour
300 g fresh or frozen raspberries
½ cup chocolate chips or carob buds
½ cup grapeseed oil
½ cup apple juice concentrate
¾ cup low-fat milk or low-fat soy milk
3 egg whites or 2 whole eggs
extra 12 chocolate chips or carob buds

MAKES 12

- Preheat the oven to 180°C and lightly grease the muffin tray.

- Sift the flours into a medium-sized bowl and add the raspberries and chocolate chips.

- In another bowl, combine the grapeseed oil, apple juice concentrate, milk and egg whites, and beat well.

- Add the egg mixture to the flour and fruit and stir thoroughly.

- Spoon into the muffin tray and top each muffin with a chocolate chip.

- Bake for 20–25 minutes or until golden brown.

- Remove the muffins immediately from the tray and allow to cool, covered with a tea towel, on a wire rack.

RASPBERRIES

The raspberry was a native of Europe before finding its way around the world. Surprisingly, it is high in fibre and iron with a significant amount of vitamin C. But its greatest appeal lies in its delicate, sweet, almost wine-like flavour.

Spices and other fruits complement the flavour of raspberries, but I must confess that muffins with just raspberries are probably my favourite of all.

1½ cups unbleached white self-raising flour
½ cup wholemeal plain flour
1 teaspoon cinnamon
¼ teaspoon ground cloves
400 g fresh or frozen raspberries
½ cup grapeseed oil
½ cup apple juice concentrate
1 cup low-fat plain yoghurt
3 egg whites or 2 whole eggs

RASPBERRY, YOGHURT & SPICE MUFFINS

MAKES 12

- Preheat the oven to 180°C and lightly grease the muffin tray.

- Sift the flours and spices into a medium-sized bowl and add the raspberries.

- In another bowl, combine the grapeseed oil, apple juice concentrate, yoghurt and egg whites, and beat well.

- Add the yoghurt mixture to the flour and fruit and stir thoroughly.

- Spoon into the muffin tray and bake for 20–25 minutes or until golden brown.

- Remove the muffins immediately from the tray and allow to cool, covered with a tea towel, on a wire rack.

RASPBERRY & PECAN STREUSEL MUFFINS

MAKES 12

1½ cups unbleached white self-raising flour
½ cup soy flour
¼ cup finely chopped pecan nuts
400 g fresh or frozen raspberries
½ cup grapeseed oil
½ cup apple juice concentrate
¾ cup low-fat milk or low-fat soy milk
3 egg whites or 2 whole eggs
2 tablespoons very finely chopped pecan nuts
2 tablespoons finely chopped shredded coconut
1 teaspoon cinnamon
1 teaspoon mixed spice

- Preheat the oven to 180°C and lightly grease the muffin tray.

- Sift the flours into a medium-sized bowl and add the ¼ cup pecan nuts and the raspberries.

- In another bowl, combine the grapeseed oil, apple juice concentrate, milk and egg whites, and beat well.

- Add the egg mixture to the flour and fruit and stir thoroughly.

- Spoon into the muffin tray.

- To make the streusel, mix together the remaining ingredients and spoon a little on to the top of each muffin.

- Bake for 20–25 minutes or until golden brown.

- Remove the muffins immediately from the tray and allow to cool, covered with a tea towel, on a wire rack. (See colour plate opposite page 42.)

OPPOSITE
Pumpkin, Oat & Poppyseed (page 93) and Corn & Herb (page 85) muffins.

1½ cups unbleached white self-raising flour
½ cup soy flour
300 g fresh or frozen raspberries
½ cup finely chopped walnuts
½ cup grapeseed oil
½ cup apple juice concentrate
1 cup low-fat milk or low-fat soy milk
3 egg whites or 2 whole eggs

- Preheat the oven to 180°C and lightly grease the muffin tray.

- Sift the flours into a medium-sized bowl and add the raspberries and walnuts.

- In another bowl, combine the grapeseed oil, apple juice concentrate, milk and egg whites, and beat well.

- Add the egg mixture to the flour and fruit and stir thoroughly.

- Spoon into the muffin tray and bake for 20–25 minutes or until golden brown.

- Remove the muffins immediately from the tray and allow to cool, covered with a tea towel, on a wire rack.

RASPBERRY & WALNUT MUFFINS

MAKES 12

OPPOSITE
Tomato, Onion & Basil Muffins
(page 98).

RHUBARB & GINGER MUFFINS

MAKES 12

RHUBARB

Many people think of rhubarb as a fruit but it is actually a vegetable related to sorrel. Only the pinkish stem of this large perennial plant is used in cooking; the leaves contain dangerous amounts of oxalic acid. Its kilojoule value is low compared to most fruits and it is significantly high in calcium.

It is not necessary to cook rhubarb before using it in muffin recipes as it becomes moist in the baking process and its sharp taste is sweetened by the apple juice concentrate. Walnuts, pecan nuts, cinnamon, mixed spice, cloves, cardamom and ginger all complement the flavour of rhubarb.

1½ cups unbleached white self-raising flour
½ cup wholemeal plain flour
1 teaspoon ground ginger
300 g rhubarb, finely chopped
¼ cup finely chopped glacé ginger
½ cup grapeseed oil
½ cup apple juice concentrate
¾ cup low-fat milk or low-fat soy milk
3 egg whites or 2 whole eggs

- Preheat the oven to 180°C and lightly grease the muffin tray.

- Sift the flours and spice into a medium-sized bowl and add the rhubarb and glacé ginger.

- In another bowl, combine the grapeseed oil, apple juice concentrate, milk and egg whites, and beat well.

- Add the egg mixture to the flour and fruit and stir thoroughly.

- Spoon into the muffin tray and bake for 20–25 minutes or until golden brown.

- Remove the muffins immediately from the tray and allow to cool, covered with a tea towel, on a wire rack.

1 cup rolled oats
2 cups oat bran
1 cup unbleached white plain flour
1½ tablespoons baking powder
1 teaspoon bicarbonate of soda
2 teaspoons cinnamon
400 g rhubarb, chopped
½ cup grapeseed oil
½ cup apple juice concentrate
1 cup low-fat milk or low-fat soy milk
2 teaspoons vanilla essence
4 egg whites or 3 whole eggs

RHUBARB, OAT & CINNAMON MUFFINS

MAKES 12

- Preheat the oven to 180°C and lightly grease the muffin tray.

- Place the rolled oats and oat bran in a medium-sized bowl and sift the flour, baking powder, bicarbonate of soda and cinnamon into it.

- Add the rhubarb to the dry ingredients and mix together.

- In another bowl, combine the grapeseed oil, apple juice concentrate, milk, vanilla essence and egg whites, and beat well.

- Add the egg mixture to the flour and fruit and stir thoroughly.

- Spoon into the muffin tray and bake for 25–30 minutes or until golden brown.

- Remove the muffins immediately from the tray and allow to cool, covered with a tea towel, on a wire rack.

RHUBARB, OAT & PINEAPPLE MUFFINS

MAKES 12

2 cups oat bran
2 cups unbleached white plain flour
1½ tablespoons baking powder
2 teaspoons cinnamon
1 x 440 g can unsweetened pineapple pieces
½ cup chopped walnuts
250 g rhubarb, finely chopped
¼ cup water
½ cup apple juice concentrate
½ cup grapeseed oil
2 teaspoons vanilla essence
3 egg whites or 2 whole eggs

- Preheat the oven to 180°C and lightly grease the muffin tray.

- Place the oat bran in a medium-sized bowl and sift the flour, baking powder and cinnamon into it. Mix together.

- Drain the pineapple, reserving ¾ cup juice, and add to the dry ingredients with the walnuts and rhubarb.

- In another bowl, combine the pineapple juice, water, apple juice concentrate, grapeseed oil, vanilla essence and egg whites, and beat well.

- Add the pineapple juice mixture to the flour and fruit and stir thoroughly.

- Spoon into the muffin tray and bake for 25–30 minutes or until golden brown.

- Remove the muffins immediately from the tray and allow to cool, covered with a tea towel, on a wire rack.

1½ cups unbleached white self-raising flour
½ cup wholemeal plain flour
1 teaspoon cinnamon
½ teaspoon mixed spice
½ cup finely chopped pecan nuts
300 g rhubarb, chopped into small chunks
½ cup grapeseed oil
½ cup apple juice concentrate
1 cup low-fat milk or low-fat soy milk
3 egg whites or 2 whole eggs
extra 12 pecan nuts, shelled

CHUNKY RHUBARB & PECAN MUFFINS

- Preheat the oven to 180°C and lightly grease the muffin tray.

- Sift the flours and spices into a medium-sized bowl and add the chopped pecan nuts and rhubarb.

- In another bowl, combine the grapeseed oil, apple juice concentrate, milk and egg whites, and beat well.

- Add the egg mixture to the flour and fruit and stir thoroughly.

- Spoon into the muffin tray and top each muffin with a pecan nut.

- Bake for 20–25 minutes or until golden brown.

- Remove the muffins immediately from the tray and allow to cool, covered with a tea towel, on a wire rack.

MAKES 12

PECAN NUTS

The pecan nut originated in North America and has become a popular addition to many American dishes. The nut is low in fibre and high in oil, the oil being 85 per cent unsaturated (mainly mono-unsaturated).

Pecan nuts impart a wonderfully rich flavour when cooked and can be added chopped to the muffin mixture or whole to the top of a muffin before cooking.

SPICY APPLE & WALNUT MUFFINS

MAKES 12

1½ cups unbleached white self-raising flour
½ cup wholemeal plain flour
1 teaspoon cinnamon
½ teaspoon mixed spice
½ teaspoon nutmeg
1 x 425 g can unsweetened apple
¾ cup chopped walnuts
½ cup grapeseed oil
½ cup apple juice concentrate
¾ cup low-fat milk or low-fat soy milk
3 egg whites or 2 whole eggs

- Preheat the oven to 180°C and lightly grease the muffin tray.

- Sift the flours and spices into a medium-sized bowl and then add the apple and walnuts.

- In another bowl, combine the grapeseed oil, apple juice concentrate, milk and egg whites, and beat well.

- Add the egg mixture to the flour and fruit and stir thoroughly.

- Spoon into the muffin tray and bake for 20–25 minutes or until golden brown.

- Remove the muffins immediately from the tray and allow to cool, covered with a tea towel, on a wire rack.

SPICY PEAR, OAT & ALMOND MUFFINS

1 cup rolled oats
2 cups oat bran
1 cup unbleached white plain flour
1½ tablespoons baking powder
3 teaspoons Spice Mixture (see below)
500 g cooked or canned unsweetened pears
  in natural juice
grated rind of 1 large lemon
½ cup apple juice concentrate
½ cup grapeseed oil
2 teaspoons vanilla essence
3 egg whites or 2 whole eggs
1½ tablespoons coarsely ground almonds

- Preheat the oven to 180°C and lightly grease the muffin tray.

- Place the rolled oats and oat bran in a medium-sized bowl and sift in the flour, baking powder and Spice Mixture.

- Drain the pears, reserving 1 cup cooking liquid or juice, and chop. Add the pear and lemon rind to the dry ingredients.

- In another bowl, combine the pear juice, apple juice concentrate, grapeseed oil, vanilla and egg whites, and beat well.

- Add the pear juice mixture to the flour and fruit, and stir thoroughly.

- Spoon into the muffin tray and sprinkle ground almonds over each muffin.

- Bake for 25–30 minutes or until golden brown.

- Remove the muffins immediately from the tray and allow to cool, covered with a tea towel, on a wire rack.

MAKES 12

SPICE MIXTURE
Combine equal quantities of cinnamon, ground cloves, ground pepper, ground ginger and ground cardamom for a delicious Spice Mixture that can be used to flavour all sorts of muffins. Stored in an airtight container, this Spice Mixture keeps well.

WHEAT-FREE APPLE & SPICE MUFFINS

MAKES 12

1 cup rice flour
½ cup soy flour
½ cup corn meal
2 teaspoons baking powder
½ teaspoon bicarbonate of soda
1 teaspoon mixed spice
1 teaspoon cinnamon
2 teaspoons finely grated orange rind
1 x 425 g can unsweetened apple
½ cup grapeseed oil
⅓ cup apple juice concentrate
1 cup low-fat milk or low-fat soy milk
3 egg whites or 2 whole eggs

- Preheat the oven to 180°C and lightly grease the muffin tray.

- Sift the flours, corn meal, baking powder, bicarbonate of soda and spices into a medium-sized bowl and add the orange rind and apple.

- In another bowl, combine the grapeseed oil, apple juice concentrate, milk and egg whites, and beat well.

- Add the egg mixture to the flour and fruit, and stir thoroughly.

- Spoon into the muffin tray and bake for 20–25 minutes or until golden brown.

- Remove the muffins immediately from the tray and allow to cool, covered with a tea towel, on a wire rack.

WHEAT-FREE BANANA & MACADAMIA NUT MUFFINS

1½ cups rice flour
½ cup soy flour
½ teaspoon bicarbonate of soda
2 teaspoons baking powder
¼ teaspoon nutmeg
½ teaspoon cinnamon
2 bananas, peeled and chopped
½ cup finely chopped macadamia nuts
½ cup grapeseed oil
½ cup apple juice concentrate
1 cup low-fat milk or low-fat soy milk
3 egg whites or 2 whole eggs

- Preheat the oven to 180°C and lightly grease the muffin tray.

- Sift the flours, bicarbonate of soda, baking powder and spices into a medium-sized bowl and add the banana and chopped macadamia nuts.

- In another bowl, combine the grapeseed oil, apple juice concentrate, milk and egg whites, and beat well.

- Add the egg mixture to the flour and fruit and stir thoroughly.

- Spoon into the muffin tray and bake for 20–25 minutes or until golden brown.

- Remove the muffins immediately from the tray and allow to cool, covered with a tea towel, on a wire rack.

MAKES 12

RICE FLOUR
Rice flour is gluten free and is milled from white or brown rice grains. It is rich in starch and fibre and gives a gritty texture to cooked muffins. Rice flour combines well with soy flour or corn meal to make gluten-free muffins.

WHEAT-FREE BLUEBERRY & APRICOT MUFFINS

1 cup rice flour
1/3 cup soy flour
1/2 cup corn meal
2 teaspoons baking powder
1/2 teaspoon bicarbonate of soda
1 teaspoon cinnamon
300 g fresh or frozen blueberries
100 g dried apricots, finely chopped
1/2 cup grapeseed oil
1/2 cup apple juice concentrate
3/4 cup low-fat milk or low-fat soy milk
4 egg whites or 3 whole eggs

- Preheat the oven to 180°C and lightly grease the muffin tray.

- Sift the flours, corn meal, baking powder, bicarbonate of soda and cinnamon into a medium-sized bowl and add the blueberries and apricots.

- In another bowl, combine the grapeseed oil, apple juice concentrate, milk and egg whites, and beat well.

- Add the egg mixture to the flour and fruit, and stir thoroughly.

- Spoon into the muffin tray and bake for 20–25 minutes or until golden brown.

- Remove the muffins immediately from the tray and allow to cool, covered with a tea towel, on a wire rack.

⅔ cup rice flour
⅔ cup soy flour
⅔ cup very finely ground almonds
2 teaspoons baking powder
½ teaspoon bicarbonate of soda
1 teaspoon finely grated orange rind
½ cup finely chopped dried apricots
½ cup mixed peel
½ cup grapeseed oil
½ cup apple juice concentrate
1 cup low-fat milk or low-fat soy milk
4 egg whites or 3 whole eggs

WHEAT-FREE CITRUS & APRICOT MUFFINS

MAKES 12

- Preheat the oven to 160°C and lightly grease the muffin tray.

- Sift the flours, ground almonds, baking powder and bicarbonate of soda into a medium-sized bowl and add the orange rind, apricot and mixed peel.

- In another bowl, combine the grapeseed oil, apple juice concentrate, milk and egg whites, and beat well.

- Add the egg mixture to the flour and fruit and stir thoroughly.

- Spoon into the muffin tray and bake for 25–30 minutes or until golden brown.

- Remove the muffins immediately from the tray and allow to cool, covered with a tea towel, on a wire rack.

WHEAT-FREE ORANGE & CHOCOLATE CHIP MUFFINS

MAKES 12

⅔ cup rice flour
⅔ cup soy flour
⅔ cup very finely ground almonds
2 teaspoons baking powder
½ teaspoon bicarbonate of soda
1 cup chocolate chips or *carob buds*
½ cup grapeseed oil
⅓ cup apple juice concentrate
1 cup fresh orange juice
4 egg whites or *3 whole eggs*

- Preheat the oven to 160°C and lightly grease the muffin tray.

- Sift the flours, ground almonds, baking powder and bicarbonate of soda into a medium-sized bowl and then add the chocolate chips.

- In another bowl, combine the grapeseed oil, apple juice concentrate, orange juice and egg whites, and beat well.

- Add the orange juice mixture to the flour and chocolate chips and stir thoroughly.

- Spoon into the muffin tray and bake for 25–30 minutes or until golden brown.

- Remove the muffins immediately from the tray and allow to cool, covered with a tea towel, on a wire rack.

⅔ cup rice flour
⅔ cup soy flour
⅔ cup very finely ground almonds
2 teaspoons baking powder
½ teaspoon bicarbonate of soda
2 teaspoons cinnamon
1 x 425 g can unsweetened peaches in
    natural juice
½ cup grapeseed oil
¼ cup low-fat milk or low-fat soy milk
3 egg whites or 2 whole eggs

- Preheat the oven to 160°C and lightly grease the muffin tray.

- Sift the flours, ground almonds, baking powder, bicarbonate of soda and spice into a medium-sized bowl.

- Drain the peaches, reserving 1 cup juice, and add to the dry ingredients.

- In another bowl, combine the peach juice, grapeseed oil, milk and egg whites, and beat well.

- Add the peach juice mixture to the flour and fruit and stir thoroughly.

- Spoon into the muffin tray and bake for 25–30 minutes or until golden brown.

- Remove the muffins immediately from the tray and allow to cool, covered with a tea towel, on a wire rack.

WHEAT-FREE PEACH & CINNAMON MUFFINS

MAKES 12

SOY FLOUR

Soy flour is processed from soya beans, which contain all eight of the essential amino acids. Soy beans are also an excellent source of protein, iron and thiamin and have a moderate amount of fibre, niacin, calcium and zinc.

I like to use one part soy to three parts other flour in muffin making. Soy flour browns faster than other flours, so if you increase the amount of soy flour in your recipes beyond the suggested amount, lower your oven temperature and cook the muffins a little longer. Another advantage of soy flour is that its lecithin content enhances the keeping quality of muffins.

WHOLEMEAL BERRY COMBO MUFFINS

MAKES 12

1 cup wholemeal self-raising flour
½ cup unbleached white self-raising flour
½ cup unbleached white plain flour
2 teaspoons cinnamon
1 cup fresh or frozen raspberries
1 cup fresh or frozen blueberries or 2 cups
    mixed berries
½ cup grapeseed oil
½ cup apple juice concentrate
¾ cup low-fat milk or low-fat soy milk
3 egg whites or 2 whole eggs

■ Preheat the oven to 180°C and lightly grease the muffin tray.

■ Sift the flours and spice into a medium-sized bowl and add the berries.

■ In another bowl, combine the grapeseed oil, apple juice concentrate, milk and egg whites, and beat well.

■ Add the egg mixture to the flour and fruit and stir thoroughly.

■ Spoon into the muffin tray and bake for 20–25 minutes or until golden brown.

■ Remove the muffins immediately from the tray and allow to cool, covered with a tea towel, on a wire rack.

1½ cups wholemeal self-raising flour
½ cup unbleached white plain flour
1 cup finely chopped dates
2 oranges, peeled, pith removed and chopped
1 teaspoon finely grated orange rind
½ cup grapeseed oil
½ cup apple juice concentrate
¾ cup fresh orange juice
3 egg whites or 2 whole eggs

- Preheat the oven to 180°C and lightly grease the muffin tray.

- Sift the flours into a medium-sized bowl and add the dates, orange and orange rind.

- In another bowl, combine the grapeseed oil, apple juice concentrate, orange juice and egg whites, and beat well.

- Add the orange juice mixture to the flour and fruit and stir thoroughly.

- Spoon into the muffin tray and bake for 20–25 minutes or until golden brown.

- Remove the muffins immediately from the tray and allow to cool, covered with a tea towel, on a wire rack.

WHOLEMEAL DATE & ORANGE MUFFINS

MAKES 12

SAVOURY MUFFINS

ASPARAGUS & OLIVE MUFFINS

ASPARAGUS

Since ancient times asparagus has been valued for its medicinal properties – it is a natural diuretic and laxative but I value it simply for its wonderful flavour.

Asparagus has significant amounts of vitamin C and vitamin E. It is available fresh from spring to summer but the canned varieties are suitable to use in muffin making. Drain the asparagus well and quickly rinse to remove any excess salt.

You'll find by adding a little grated orange rind or nutmeg or herbs such as chives, lemon balm, sage, tarragon or thyme, your asparagus muffins will have a different flavour every time.

1½ cups unbleached white self-raising flour
½ cup wholemeal plain flour
2 x 340 g cans asparagus pieces, drained
¼ cup finely chopped black olives
½ cup grapeseed oil
1½ cups low-fat milk or low-fat soy milk
3 egg whites or 2 whole eggs

- Preheat the oven to 180°C and lightly grease the muffin tray.

- Sift the flours into a medium-sized bowl and add the asparagus and olives.

- In another bowl, combine the grapeseed oil, milk and egg whites, and beat well.

- Add the egg mixture to the flour and stir thoroughly.

- Spoon into the muffin tray and bake for 20–25 minutes or until golden brown.

- Remove the muffins immediately from the tray and allow to cool, covered with a tea towel, on a wire rack.

1½ cups unbleached white self-raising flour
½ cup unbleached white plain flour
2 x 340 g cans asparagus pieces
¼ cup freshly grated parmesan cheese
¼ cup finely chopped fresh chives or parsley
¾ cup grated carrot
½ cup grapeseed oil
3 egg whites or 2 whole eggs
2 tablespoons sesame seeds (optional)

- Preheat the oven to 180°C and lightly grease the muffin tray.

- Sift the flours into a medium-sized bowl.

- Drain the asparagus, reserving ¾ cup juice, and add to the flour with the cheese, chives and carrot.

- In another bowl, combine the asparagus juice, grapeseed oil and egg whites, and beat well.

- Add the asparagus juice mixture to the flour and stir thoroughly.

- Spoon into the muffin tray and sprinkle sesame seeds on top of each muffin, if desired.

- Bake for 20–25 minutes or until golden brown.

- Remove the muffins immediately from the tray and allow to cool, covered with a tea towel, on a wire rack.

ASPARAGUS, CARROT & CHEESE MUFFINS

MAKES 12

CARROT & PINEAPPLE MUFFINS

MAKES 12

1½ cups unbleached white self-raising flour
½ cup wholemeal plain flour
1½ teaspoons cinnamon
1 x 440 g can crushed unsweetened pineapple
   in natural juice
½ cup grated and firmly packed carrot
½ cup grapeseed oil
2 tablespoons apple juice concentrate
½ cup low-fat milk or low-fat soy milk
2 teaspoons vanilla essence
3 egg whites or 2 whole eggs

- Preheat the oven to 180°C and lightly grease the muffin tray.

- Sift the flours and spice into a medium-sized bowl.

- Drain the pineapple, reserving 1 cup juice, and add to the flour with the carrot.

- In another bowl, combine the pineapple juice, grapeseed oil, apple juice concentrate, milk, vanilla essence and egg whites, and beat well.

- Add the pineapple juice mixture to the flour and stir thoroughly.

- Spoon into the muffin tray and bake for 20–25 minutes or until golden brown.

- Remove the muffins immediately from the tray and allow to cool, covered with a tea towel, on a wire rack.

1½ cups unbleached white self-raising flour
½ cup wholemeal plain flour
1 cup grated carrot
¾ cup freshly grated parmesan cheese
1 tablespoon finely chopped fresh parsley
    or chives
1 tablespoon grainy mustard
½ cup grapeseed oil
1½ cups low-fat milk or low-fat soy milk
4 egg whites or 3 whole eggs

- Preheat the oven to 180°C and lightly grease the muffin tray.

- Sift the flours into a medium-sized bowl and add the carrot, cheese and parsley.

- In another bowl, combine the mustard, grapeseed oil, milk and egg whites, and beat well.

- Add the mustard mixture to the flour and stir thoroughly.

- Spoon into the muffin tray and bake for 20–25 minutes or until golden brown.

- Remove the muffins immediately from the tray and allow to cool, covered with a tea towel, on a wire rack.

CARROT, CHEESE & MUSTARD MUFFINS

MAKES 12

WHOLEMEAL FLOUR
This flour is milled from the whole wheat grain with a large proportion of the outer husk remaining in the finished product. It adds texture, a nutty flavour, and essential fibre to your muffins. Wholemeal flour contains more minerals and vitamins than white flour. It is an excellent source of niacin, iron and magnesium, with smaller amounts of protein and zinc.

CARROT, OAT & COCONUT MUFFINS

MAKES 12

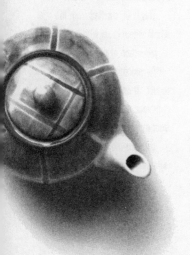

2 cups oat bran
2 cups wholemeal plain flour
1½ tablespoons baking powder
400 g carrots
200 g raisins
½ cup shredded coconut
1 cup low-fat milk
2 teaspoons vanilla essence
½ cup grapeseed oil
½ cup apple juice concentrate
3 egg whites

■ Preheat the oven to 180°C and lightly grease the muffin tray.

■ Place the oat bran in a medium-sized bowl and sift the flour and baking powder into it. Mix together.

■ Juice the carrots to give approximately 1 cup juice and 150 g pulp.

■ In another bowl, combine the carrot juice, pulp and raisins.

■ Process the coconut and milk in a blender and add to the carrot mixture with the vanilla essence, grapeseed oil and apple juice concentrate. Beat well.

■ Add the flour and oats to the carrot mixture in three lots, stirring each time.

■ Beat the egg whites until stiff and gently fold through the mixture.

■ Spoon into the muffin tray and bake for 25–30 minutes or until golden brown.

■ Remove the muffins immediately from the tray and allow to cool, covered with a tea towel, on a wire rack.

2 cups oat bran
1 cup rolled oats
1 cup unbleached white plain flour
1½ tablespoons baking powder
400 g carrots
125 g glacé ginger, chopped
100 g dried apricots, chopped
½ cup grapeseed oil
½ cup apple juice concentrate
grated rind of 2 lemons
4 egg whites

CARROT, OAT & GINGER MUFFINS

MAKES 12

- Preheat the oven to 180°C and lightly grease the muffin tray.

- Combine the oat bran and rolled oats in a medium-sized bowl and sift in the flour and baking powder. Mix together.

- Juice the carrots to give approximately 1 cup juice and 150 g pulp.

- In another bowl, combine the carrot juice and pulp with the remaining ingredients, except the egg whites, and beat thoroughly.

- Add the flour and oats to the carrot mixture in three lots, stirring each time.

- Beat the egg whites until stiff and gently fold through the mixture.

- Spoon into the muffin tray and bake for 25–30 minutes or until golden brown.

- Remove the muffins immediately from the tray and allow to cool, covered with a tea towel, on a wire rack.

CARROT, OAT & MIXED PEEL MUFFINS

MAKES 12

2 cups oat bran
2 cups unbleached white plain flour
1½ tablespoons baking powder
1 teaspoon cinnamon
1 teaspoon mixed spice
400 g carrots
½ cup apple juice concentrate
½ cup grapeseed oil
200 g mixed peel
2 teaspoons vanilla essence
grated rind of 2 oranges
4 egg whites

- Preheat the oven to 180°C and lightly grease the muffin tray.

- Place the oat bran in a medium-sized bowl and sift the flour, baking powder and spices into it. Mix together.

- Juice the carrots to give approximately 1 cup juice and 150 g pulp.

- In another bowl, combine the carrot juice and pulp, apple juice concentrate, grapeseed oil, mixed peel, vanilla essence and orange rind. Beat well.

- Add the flour and oat mixture to the carrot mixture in three lots, stirring each time.

- Beat the egg whites until stiff and gently fold through the mixture.

- Spoon into the muffin tray and bake for 25–30 minutes or until golden brown.

- Remove the muffins immediately from the tray and allow to cool, covered with a tea towel, on a wire rack.

CHEESY CORN-MEAL MUFFINS

½ cup corn meal
1½ cups unbleached white self-raising flour
1 cup freshly grated parmesan cheese
2 teaspoons dried dill
½ cup grapeseed oil
1½ cups low-fat milk or low-fat soy milk
4 egg whites or 3 whole eggs

MAKES 12

- Preheat the oven to 180°C and lightly grease the muffin tray.

- Place the corn meal into a medium-sized bowl and sift in the flour. Mix together.

- Add the cheese and dill to the flour and corn meal.

- In another bowl, combine the grapeseed oil, milk and egg whites and beat well.

- Add the egg mixture to the flour and stir thoroughly.

- Spoon into the muffin tray and bake for 20–25 minutes or until golden brown.

- Remove the muffins immediately from the tray and allow to cool, covered with a tea towel, on a wire rack.

CORN MEAL

Corn meal is a yellow, granular flour made from corn. It is a good source of thiamin and iron and contains a smaller amount of protein and niacin. The coarse, stone-ground corn meal will give your muffins a gritty texture (you may need to add a little extra liquid); the finer, yellow corn meal will give your muffins a soft, smooth texture.

CORN & SUN-DRIED TOMATO MUFFINS

MAKES 12

1½ cups unbleached white self-raising flour
¾ cup unbleached white plain flour
½ cup freshly grated parmesan cheese
1½ cups cooked corn kernels
½ cup finely chopped sun-dried tomatoes
½ cup grapeseed oil
1 cup low-fat milk or low-fat soy milk
4 egg whites or 3 whole eggs

- Preheat the oven to 180°C and lightly grease the muffin tray.

- Sift the flours into a medium-sized bowl and add the cheese, corn and tomato.

- In another bowl, combine the grapeseed oil, milk and egg whites, and beat well.

- Add the egg mixture to the flour and stir thoroughly.

- Spoon into the muffin tray and bake for 20–25 minutes or until golden brown.

- Remove the muffins immediately from the tray and allow to cool, covered with a tea towel, on a wire rack.

1½ cups unbleached white self-raising flour
¾ cup unbleached white plain flour
¾ cup grated low-fat mozzarella cheese
1½ cups cooked corn kernels
½ cup finely chopped fresh herbs (e.g. basil,
   parsley, chives, oregano and thyme)
½ cup grapeseed oil
1 cup low-fat milk or low-fat soy milk
4 egg whites or 3 whole eggs

CORN & HERB MUFFINS

MAKES 12

- Preheat the oven to 180°C and lightly grease the muffin tray.

- Sift the flours into a medium-sized bowl and add the cheese, corn and herbs.

- In another bowl, combine the grapeseed oil, milk and egg whites, and beat well.

- Add the egg mixture to the flour and stir thoroughly.

- Spoon into the muffin tray and bake for 20–25 minutes or until golden brown.

- Remove the muffins immediately from the tray and allow to cool, covered with a tea towel, on a wire rack. (See colour plate opposite page 58.)

CORN

Corn originated in America and although commonly called a vegetable, it is actually the seed of a type of grass, so it is also classed as a cereal. It is a good source of fibre, phosphorus, thiamin and niacin.

The small, sweet, yellow kernels are cut from the ear of the corn for use in corn muffins. When fresh corn is not available, used canned corn. Drain it well and rinse to remove any excess salt from the canning liquid.

Surprisingly, corn and banana go well together, but my favourite combination is corn, spring onion, lots of dill and a little sharp-tasting cheese.

CRAB & SUN-DRIED TOMATO MUFFINS

MAKES 12

1½ cups unbleached white self-raising flour
½ cup wholemeal plain flour
1 x 200 g can crab meat, drained
¾ cup freshly grated parmesan cheese
1 teaspoon dried dill
⅓ cup finely chopped sun-dried tomatoes
½ cup grapeseed oil
1½ cups low-fat milk or low-fat soy milk
4 egg whites or 3 whole eggs

- Preheat the oven to 180°C and lightly grease the muffin tray.

- Sift the flours into a medium-sized bowl and add the crab, cheese, dill and tomato.

- In another bowl, combine the grapeseed oil, milk and egg whites, and beat well.

- Add the egg mixture to the flour and stir thoroughly.

- Spoon into the muffin tray and bake for 20–25 minutes or until golden brown.

- Remove the muffins immediately from the tray and allow to cool, covered with a tea towel, on a wire rack.

1 cup boiling water
½ cup sultanas
1½ cups unbleached white self-raising flour
½ cup soy flour
2 bananas, peeled and finely chopped
1 tablespoon vindaloo curry paste
½ cup grapeseed oil
1½ cups low-fat milk or low-fat soy milk
3 egg whites or 2 whole eggs

- Pour boiling water over the sultanas in a bowl and leave to stand for 10 minutes. Drain.

- Preheat the oven to 180°C and lightly grease the muffin tray.

- Sift the flours into a medium-sized bowl and add the sultanas and banana.

- In another bowl, combine the curry paste, grapeseed oil, milk and egg whites, and beat well.

- Add the curry mixture to the flour and fruit and stir thoroughly.

- Spoon into the muffin tray and bake for 20–25 minutes or until golden brown.

- Remove the muffins immediately from the tray and allow to cool, covered with a tea towel, on a wire rack.

CURRY, BANANA & SULTANA MUFFINS

MAKES 12

CURRY, CHEESE & CELERY MUFFINS

MAKES 12

1½ cups unbleached white self-raising flour
½ cup wholemeal plain flour
1 cup freshly grated parmesan cheese
¾ cup finely chopped celery
1 tablespoon vindaloo curry paste
½ cup grapeseed oil
1½ cups low-fat milk or low-fat soy milk
4 egg whites or 3 whole eggs

- Preheat the oven to 180°C and lightly grease the muffin tray.

- Sift the flours into a medium-sized bowl and add the cheese and celery.

- In another bowl, combine the curry paste, grapeseed oil, milk and egg whites, and beat well.

- Add the curry mixture to the flour and stir thoroughly.

- Spoon into the muffin tray and bake for 20–25 minutes or until golden brown.

- Remove the muffins immediately from the tray and allow to cool, covered with a tea towel, on a wire rack.

1½ cups unbleached white self-raising flour
½ cup bran
pinch of cayenne pepper
400 g mushrooms
½ cup fresh basil leaves
½ cup grapeseed oil
1½ cups low-fat milk or low-fat soy milk
3 egg whites or 2 whole eggs

MUSHROOM & BASIL MUFFINS

MAKES 12

- Preheat the oven to 180°C and lightly grease the muffin tray.

- Sift the flour into a medium-sized bowl and add the bran and cayenne pepper.

- Mince the mushrooms and basil in a food processor and add to the flour.

- In another bowl, combine the grapeseed oil, milk and egg whites, and beat well.

- Add the egg mixture to the flour and mushrooms and stir thoroughly.

- Spoon into the muffin tray and bake for 25–30 minutes or until golden brown.

- Remove the muffins immediately from the tray and allow to cool, covered with a tea towel, on a wire rack.

MUSHROOMS

Mushrooms contain a valuable number of B group vitamins and are high in iron. They are also a good source of pantothenic acid, niacin, riboflavin and phosphorus.

In savoury muffins mushrooms combine well with individual herbs such as basil or dill, or with mixed herbs. They can be added to the muffin mixture raw or cooked.

PEAR, CHEESE & PINENUT MUFFINS

MAKES 12

PEARS

There are said to be over 5000 different varieties of pear worldwide. The most commonly known and most popular cooking pear is the Williams or Bartlett variety.

Pears are high in kilojoules compared to most other fruits, with the major nutrient being vitamin C. Both fresh or canned pears can be used in your muffin recipes. Soak them in sherry, port, marsala or rum to enhance their flavour before cooking, or choose a spice such as cinnamon, cardamom, ginger or cloves to add an aromatic touch.

1½ cups unbleached white self-raising flour
½ cup wholemeal plain flour
pinch of cayenne pepper
½ cup freshly grated parmesan cheese
3 medium-ripe pears, peeled, cored and finely chopped
½ cup grapeseed oil
1 cup low-fat milk or low-fat soy milk
4 egg whites or 3 whole eggs
¼ cup pinenuts

- Preheat the oven to 180°C and lightly grease the muffin tray.

- Sift the flours and spice into a medium-sized bowl and add the cheese and pear.

- In another bowl, combine the grapeseed oil, milk and egg whites, and beat well.

- Add the egg mixture to the flour and stir thoroughly.

- Spoon into the muffin tray and top each muffin with a few pinenuts.

- Bake for 20–25 minutes or until golden brown.

- Remove the muffins immediately from the tray and allow to cool, covered with a tea towel, on a wire rack.

4 potatoes, peeled and chopped
1 cup freshly grated parmesan cheese
1 cup finely chopped spring onions
1 teaspoon dried mixed herbs or 2 tablespoons
   finely chopped fresh herbs
1½ cups low-fat milk or low-fat soy milk
½ cup grapeseed oil
3 egg whites or 2 whole eggs
1½ cups unbleached white self-raising flour
½ cup wholemeal plain flour

POTATO & HERB MUFFINS

MAKES 12

- Cook the potatoes until tender. Drain, mash and leave to cool.

- Preheat the oven to 180°C and lightly grease the muffin tray.

- Place the cooled potatoes in a medium-sized bowl and add the cheese, spring onion and herbs.

- In another bowl, combine the milk, grapeseed oil and egg whites, and beat well.

- Add the egg mixture to the potato and stir thoroughly.

- Sift the flours into the potato mixture in two lots, stirring each time.

- Spoon into the muffin tray and bake for 25–30 minutes or until golden brown.

- Remove the muffins immediately from the tray and allow to cool, covered with a tea towel, on a wire rack.

PUMPKIN & APRICOT MUFFINS

MAKES 12

500 g pumpkin, peeled and chopped
1½ cups unbleached white self-raising flour
½ cup wholemeal plain flour
1 teaspoon cinnamon
1 cup finely chopped dried apricots
½ cup grapeseed oil
½ cup apple juice concentrate
½ cup low-fat milk or low-fat soy milk
3 egg whites or 2 whole eggs
12 pecan nuts (optional)

- Cook the pumpkin until tender. Drain, mash and leave to cool.

- Preheat the oven to 180°C and lightly grease the muffin tray.

- Sift the flours and spice into a medium-sized bowl and add the dried apricots.

- In another bowl, combine the pumpkin, grapeseed oil, apple juice concentrate, milk and egg whites, and beat well.

- Add the pumpkin mixture to the flour and stir thoroughly.

- Spoon into the muffin tray and top each muffin with a pecan nut, if desired.

- Bake for 20–25 minutes or until golden brown.

- Remove the muffins immediately from the tray and allow to cool, covered with a tea towel, on a wire rack.

PUMPKIN

The pumpkin originated in South America. Although most often used in savoury dishes its sweetness lends itself to cakes and muffins, and its moisture adds to their keeping qualities. Interesting flavours can be achieved by combining pumpkin with spices or nuts such as cinnamon, nutmeg, cardamom, cloves and walnuts.

Pumpkin can be cooked, mashed and then added to your muffin mixture or grated raw and added. The pumpkin is an excellent source of vitamin A, with smaller amounts of vitamin C, folate and pantothenic acid.

500 g pumpkin, peeled and chopped
2 cups oat bran
100 g poppyseeds
2 cups soy flour or unbleached white plain flour
1½ tablespoons baking powder
½ teaspoon nutmeg
1 tablespoon grated lemon or orange rind
1 cup low-fat milk or low-fat soy milk
½ cup grapeseed oil
½ cup apple juice concentrate
1 teaspoon vanilla essence
3 egg whites or 2 whole eggs

PUMPKIN, OAT & POPPYSEED MUFFINS

MAKES 12

- Cook the pumpkin until tender. Drain, mash and leave to cool.

- Preheat the oven to 180°C and lightly grease the muffin tray.

- Place the oat bran and poppyseeds in a medium-sized bowl and sift the flour, baking powder and nutmeg into it. Add the lemon rind and mix together.

- In another bowl, combine the pumpkin, milk, grapeseed oil, apple juice concentrate, vanilla essence and egg whites, and beat well.

- Add the pumpkin mixture to the flour and oat bran and stir thoroughly.

- Spoon into the muffin tray and bake for 25–30 minutes or until golden brown.

- Remove the muffins immediately from the tray and allow to cool, covered with a tea towel, on a wire rack. (See colour plate opposite page 58.)

PUMPKIN, OAT & PRUNE MUFFINS

MAKES 12

500 g pumpkin, peeled and chopped
2 cups oat bran
¾ cup rolled oats
1¼ cups unbleached white plain flour
1 teaspoon cinnamon
1 teaspoon mixed spice
½ teaspoon nutmeg
1½ tablespoons baking powder
200 g moist prunes, stoned and chopped
1 generous tablespoon grated lemon rind
1 cup fresh or unsweetened orange juice
½ cup apple juice concentrate
½ cup grapeseed oil
1 teaspoon vanilla essence
3 egg whites or 2 whole eggs

- Cook the pumpkin until tender. Drain, mash and leave to cool.

- Preheat the oven to 180°C and lightly grease the muffin tray.

- Place the oat bran and rolled oats in a medium-sized bowl and sift the flour, spices and baking powder into it. Add the prunes and lemon rind and mix together.

- In another bowl, combine the pumpkin, orange juice, apple juice concentrate, grapeseed oil, vanilla essence and egg whites, and beat well.

- Add the pumpkin mixture to the flour and oat bran and stir thoroughly.

- Spoon into the muffin tray and bake for 25–30 minutes or until golden brown.

- Remove the muffins immediately from the tray and allow to cool, covered with a tea towel, on a wire rack.

1½ cups unbleached white self-raising flour
½ cup unbleached white plain flour
¼ cup freshly chopped chives
½ cup freshly grated parmesan cheese
1 x 210 g can salmon, drained
2 tablespoons capers
½ cup grapeseed oil
1½ cups low-fat milk or low-fat soy milk
4 egg whites or 3 whole eggs

SALMON & CAPER MUFFINS

MAKES 12

- Preheat the oven to 180°C and lightly grease the muffin tray.

- Sift the flours into a medium-sized bowl and add the chives, cheese, salmon and capers.

- In another bowl, combine the grapeseed oil, milk and egg whites, and beat well.

- Add the egg mixture to the flour and stir thoroughly.

- Spoon into the muffin tray and bake for 20–25 minutes or until golden brown.

- Remove the muffins immediately from the tray and allow to cool, covered with a tea towel, on a wire rack.

SWEET POTATO & MAPLE MUFFINS

MAKES 12

SWEET POTATO

There are two types of sweet potato — the white and the red. I particularly like the sweet flavour, the vibrant orange colour and the moistness of the red variety in my muffins.

Sweet potatoes are rich in vitamin C and E and have moderate amounts of thiamin, folate and pantothenic acid. Spices such as cinnamon, mixed spice, nutmeg, cardamom and cloves complement the flavour of sweet potato and a little grated orange rind gives a tangy edge.

500 g sweet potato, peeled and chopped
1½ cups unbleached white self-raising flour
½ cup wholemeal plain flour
1 teaspoon cinnamon
½ cup finely chopped raisins
½ cup grapeseed oil
½ cup maple syrup
1 cup fresh orange juice
3 egg whites or 2 whole eggs

■ Cook the sweet potato until tender. Drain, mash and leave to cool.

■ Preheat the oven to 180°C and lightly grease the muffin tray.

■ Sift the flours and spice into a medium-sized bowl and add the raisins.

■ In another bowl, combine the grapeseed oil, maple syrup, orange juice and egg whites, and beat well.

■ Add the maple syrup mixture to the flour and stir thoroughly.

■ Spoon into the muffin tray and bake for 25–30 minutes or until golden brown.

■ Remove the muffins immediately from the tray and allow to cool, covered with a tea towel, on a wire rack.

1½ cups unbleached white self-raising flour
½ cup wholemeal plain flour
½ cup freshly grated parmesan cheese
½ cup finely chopped sun-dried tomatoes
½ cup finely chopped olives
½ cup grapeseed oil
1 cup low-fat milk or low-fat soy milk
4 egg whites or 3 whole eggs

- Preheat the oven to 180°C and lightly grease the muffin tray.

- Sift the flours into a medium-sized bowl and add the cheese, tomato and olives.

- In another bowl, combine the grapeseed oil, milk and egg whites, and beat well.

- Add the egg mixture to the flour and stir thoroughly.

- Spoon into the muffin tray and bake for 20–25 minutes or until golden brown.

- Remove the muffins immediately from the tray and allow to cool, covered with a tea towel, on a wire rack.

SUN-DRIED TOMATO & OLIVE MUFFINS

MAKES 12

TOMATO, ONION & BASIL MUFFINS

MAKES 12

1½ cups unbleached white self-raising flour
½ cup wholemeal plain flour
2 tablespoons finely chopped fresh basil
1 cup finely chopped spring onions
¼ cup finely chopped sun-dried tomatoes
½ cup grapeseed oil
1 cup salt-free tomato juice
½ cup low-fat milk or low-fat soy milk
4 egg whites or 3 whole eggs
6 cherry tomatoes, cut in half

- Preheat the oven to 180°C and lightly grease the muffin tray.

- Sift the flours into a medium-sized bowl and then add the basil, spring onion and tomato.

- In another bowl, combine the grapeseed oil, tomato juice, milk and egg whites, and beat well.

- Add the tomato juice mixture to the flour and stir thoroughly.

- Spoon into the muffin tray and place half a cherry tomato on top of each muffin, cut-side up.

- Bake for 20–25 minutes or until golden brown.

- Remove the muffins immediately from the tray and allow to cool, covered with a tea towel, on a wire rack. (See colour plate opposite page 59.)

1½ cups unbleached white self-raising flour
½ cup wholemeal plain flour
½ cup finely chopped walnuts
½ cup freshly grated parmesan cheese
¼ cup pesto
½ cup grapeseed oil
1½ cups low-fat milk or low-fat soy milk
4 egg whites or 3 whole eggs
2 tablespoons sesame seeds (optional)

- Preheat the oven to 180°C and lightly grease the muffin tray.

- Sift the flours into a medium-sized bowl and add the walnuts and cheese.

- In another bowl, combine the pesto, grapeseed oil, milk and egg whites, and beat well.

- Add the pesto mixture to the flour and stir thoroughly.

- Spoon into the muffin tray and sprinkle the top of each muffin with sesame seeds, if desired.

- Bake for 20–25 minutes or until golden brown.

- Remove the muffins immediately from the tray and allow to cool, covered with a tea towel, on a wire rack.

WALNUT & PESTO MUFFINS

MAKES 12

PESTO

Pesto comes from the Italian word *pestare*, meaning to pound or bruise, and is a thick sauce made by grinding garlic, basil, parmesan cheese, olive oil and pinenuts together. You can make your own pesto using a mortar and pestle or a food processor. The latter method is quicker but the flavour will be slightly different. There are many commercial varieties of pesto now available in the supermarket. Because of the cheese and oil content, pesto is quite high in fat so use it sparingly.

WHEAT-FREE SAVOURY SALMON MUFFINS

MAKES 12

1½ cups rice flour
½ cup corn meal
2 teaspoons baking powder
½ cup freshly grated parmesan cheese
¼ cup finely chopped fresh parsley and chives
1 x 210 g can salmon, drained
1 cup grated carrot
½ cup grapeseed oil
1½ cups low-fat milk or low-fat soy milk
4 egg whites or 3 whole eggs

- Preheat the oven to 180°C and lightly grease the muffin tray.

- Sift the flour, corn meal and baking powder into a medium-sized bowl and add the cheese, herbs, salmon and carrot.

- In another bowl, combine the grapeseed oil, milk and egg whites, and beat well.

- Add the egg mixture to the flour and stir thoroughly.

- Spoon into the muffin tray and bake for 20–25 minutes or until golden brown.

- Remove the muffins immediately from the tray and allow to cool, covered with a tea towel, on a wire rack.

1½ cups rice flour
½ cup corn meal
2 teaspoons baking powder
½ cup freshly grated parmesan cheese
2 teaspoons dried dill
1 x 210 g can tuna, drained
1 cup finely chopped celery
½ cup grapeseed oil
1½ cups low-fat milk or low-fat soy milk
4 egg whites or 3 whole eggs

- Preheat the oven to 180°C and lightly grease the muffin tray.

- Sift the flour, corn meal and baking powder into a medium-sized bowl and add the cheese, dill, tuna and celery.

- In another bowl, combine the grapeseed oil, milk and egg whites, and beat well.

- Add the egg mixture to the flour and stir thoroughly.

- Spoon into the muffin tray and bake for 20–25 minutes or until golden brown.

- Remove the muffins immediately from the tray and allow to cool, covered with a tea towel, on a wire rack.

WHEAT-FREE TUNA & CELERY MUFFINS

MAKES 12

BAKING POWDER

This fine, white powder, high in sodium but unlike bicarbonate of soda, is an excellent source of calcium and phosphorus. When heated it gives off carbon dioxide that causes the mixture to which it has been added to become aerated or light in texture.

For a sodium-free baking powder combine the following: 2 tablespoons each of cornflour, cream of tartar and potassium bicarbonate (available at chemists). Store this mixture in an airtight container and use about 2 teaspoons for every cup of flour. Many health food stores now sell this product.

ZUCCHINI & SUN-DRIED TOMATO MUFFINS

MAKES 12

1½ cups unbleached white self-raising flour
½ cup wholemeal plain flour
pinch of cayenne pepper
¼ cup freshly grated parmesan cheese
1½ cups grated and firmly packed zucchini
¼ cup finely chopped sun-dried tomatoes
½ cup grapeseed oil
1½ cups low-fat milk or low-fat soy milk
4 egg whites or 3 whole eggs

- Preheat the oven to 180°C and lightly grease the muffin tray.

- Sift the flours and cayenne pepper into a medium-sized bowl and add the cheese, zucchini and tomato.

- In another bowl, combine the grapeseed oil, milk and egg whites, and beat well.

- Add the egg mixture to the flour and stir thoroughly.

- Spoon into the muffin tray and bake for 20–25 minutes or until golden brown.

- Remove the muffins immediately from the tray and allow to cool, covered with a tea towel, on a wire rack.

1½ cups unbleached white self-raising flour
½ cup soy flour
1 teaspoon mixed spice
1½ cups grated and firmly packed zucchini
½ cup finely chopped walnuts
½ cup grapeseed oil
½ cup apple juice concentrate
1 cup low-fat milk or low-fat soy milk
3 egg whites or 2 whole eggs

ZUCCHINI & WALNUT MUFFINS

MAKES 12

- Preheat the oven to 180°C and lightly grease the muffin tray.

- Sift the flours and spice into a medium-sized bowl and then add the zucchini and walnuts.

- In another bowl, combine the grapeseed oil, apple juice concentrate, milk and egg whites, and beat well.

- Add the egg mixture to the flour and stir thoroughly.

- Spoon into the muffin tray and bake for 20–25 minutes or until golden brown.

- Remove the muffins immediately from the tray and allow to cool, covered with a tea towel, on a wire rack.

INDEX